"Don't give anyone
You need to ge...

PROMOTION READY IN 3 MONTHS

THE WOMEN'S GUIDE TO CAREER ADVANCEMENT

TABATHA K. JONES

ISBN: 9798335485098

Dedication

To the best leadership team I've ever been blessed to be a part of, my "Fab 4" work besties—Lisa, Amy, and Debbie—who taught me the art of leadership and always had my back. Lisa, you took a chance on hiring me, and I'll never forget it.

To Steve, you were the first leader to ever create space for me to speak, literally asking someone to stop talking to make room for my voice. Your leadership has been an inspiration and has made me the leader I am today. I once told you I would follow you anywhere, and this is still true today.

To Jeanne, who was the first leader to see my potential and push me to do things I never dreamed of.

To my husband, son, and Lady Tribe of friends, thank you for believing in me even when I doubted myself. Your love and support mean the world to me.

To my incredible clients, who trust me with one of the most important areas of their lives. Your journeys inspire me every day, and I love that we have become friends through this journey.

And to all the women reading this book—thank you for inviting me along on your career adventure. Let's make it a wild and wonderful ride to the top!

PREFACE

Personal Motivation and Background

Welcome to "Promotion Ready in 3 Months: The Women's Career Advancement Guide." I'm thrilled to share this journey with you. My career has been filled with ups and downs, from climbing the corporate ladder and discovering my passion for coaching to leaving my career at the age of 50 to start my entrepreneurial journey. Over the past 20+ years, I've faced many of the same challenges you might be experiencing—self-doubt, missed opportunities, and the frustration of being overlooked for promotions. These experiences ignited my passion to help women navigate their careers more strategically and effectively. And just so you know, this book will have a whole lot of authenticity because, let's face it, we all need a good laugh and a real connection to keep us going sometimes.

Purpose of the Book

This book is designed to simplify your path to career advancement and help you become a more impactful and influential leader. My goal is to provide you with actionable strategies that you can implement easily and that will have a lasting impact. Whether you aim to climb higher within your current organization, transition to a new career, or become a more influential leader, this guide will provide you with the tools you need to succeed. The book is structured into three key phases: identifying and clearing career obstacles, elevating your confidence and visibility, and articulating your value and preparing for promotions.

Acknowledging the Challenge of Asking for Help

Let's be real for a moment—asking for help is hard. As women, we often worry that reaching out will be seen as a sign of weakness. We strive to be the ones who have it all together, who can juggle a million things without breaking a sweat. This book is the help you won't ask for but absolutely deserve. It's your guide to navigating those tricky career challenges without having to raise your hand and say, "I need help."

Overview of the Challenges

Despite significant progress in workplace equality, women continue to face unique challenges in their careers. From gender biases and leadership stereotypes to balancing personal and professional responsibilities, these obstacles can hinder our growth. Through this guide, I want to address these issues head-on and empower you to overcome them.

The Empowered Leadership Coaching Program

The strategies and insights in this book are drawn from my exclusive Empowered Leadership Group Coaching Program, a transformative journey tailored to help women achieve their career advancement goals faster. I've refined this program over the years, helping numerous women become more powerfully positioned for career advancement. It's designed to help you become better positioned as a promotion-ready leader in just three months, with practical exercises, real-life success stories, and a focus on continuous growth. Once you finish reading this book, I invite you to explore the program at www.empowered-leader.com and book a call with me if you would like to continue to receive support.

Importance of Small Actions

One of the key lessons I've learned is the power of small, consistent actions. Career advancement doesn't happen overnight. It's the result of strategic planning, continuous learning, and resilience. This book encourages you to take small steps every day, to reflect on your progress, and to celebrate your achievements, no matter how small they may seem.

So, let's dive in, have a few laughs, and make some real progress together. Thank you for choosing my book to be part of your career journey. Let's transform your career and unlock the leadership potential within you.

Warm regards,
Tabatha

CONTENTS

ACKNOWLEDGMENTS

Writing "Promotion Ready in 3 Months: The Women's Guide to Career Advancement" has been an incredible journey, made possible by the support, encouragement, and contributions of many remarkable individuals.

First and foremost, I extend my deepest gratitude to the incredible women I have had the privilege to coach over the years. Your resilience, determination, and willingness to embrace new strategies have inspired this book. Your stories of transformation and success are the heart and soul of this guide.

A special thank you to my family and friends for their unwavering support and understanding throughout this process. To my husband, your encouragement and steadfast support as I transitioned from my corporate career to follow my passion for coaching have been my anchor. To my son, your constant support, encouragement, and celebration of the small wins remind me daily of the importance of pursuing dreams and achieving goals.

To my lady tribe, who keeps me grounded and adds a layer of fun and authenticity to my life, thank you for being an incredible support system. Your laughter, love, and genuine friendship are invaluable.

To my professional network and colleagues, thank you for your insights, feedback, and encouragement. Your expertise has helped shape this book into a comprehensive guide that I hope will empower women to achieve their career goals.

I am deeply grateful to my mentors and coaches who have guided me throughout my own career journey. Your wisdom and advice have been invaluable, and I am honored to pass on the knowledge I have gained from you to others.

To the readers of this book, thank you for embarking on this journey with me. Your commitment to personal and professional growth is inspiring. I hope that the strategies and stories shared in this book provide you with the tools and confidence to advance your career and achieve your goals.

Lastly, to everyone who believed in this project and contributed in ways big and small, your support has been deeply appreciated. This book is a testament to the power of collaboration, perseverance, and the collective effort to empower women in their careers.

Thank you all for being part of this journey.

With gratitude, Tabatha

"Stop waiting. To move forward in your career, get back in the driver's seat, take control, and don't allow anyone else to drive your path."

– Tabatha

CHAPTER 1

Empower Your Path – Eliminating Career Myths and Thriving

Ladies, let's chat about a myth that's been hanging around for way too long. You've heard it before: "If you want to advance your career, you have to keep your head down and work harder than anyone else." If you're a Gen-X lady like me, I'm pretty sure this was ingrained in us since birth. While hard work is definitely important, it can also be exhausting and often keeps your leadership skills hidden like a pair of Spanx under a little black dress.

The real secret to career advancement, surprisingly, is working strategically. But why do so many of us struggle to grasp this crucial truth? And why has no one ever told us?

When you look around at the women you work with, do you ever ask yourself: Why do we stay quiet and avoid sharing our successes? Why do we allow the smallest mistake to send us into a spiral of self-doubt? Why do we stay hidden behind our computers, grinding away, hoping someone else will advocate for us or magically offer us a promotion? Why do we feel like we have to be perfect before we'll even try?

How many times have you been overlooked for a promotion, knowing that you worked harder than any other candidate? How many classes, courses, and continuing education units have you taken, believing that's the way to get promoted? How many times have you taken on more responsibility, hoping your boss would notice and realize you're ready for that big promotion? How many times have you built up the courage to talk to your boss about a promotion you know you deserved only to be told – you are not ready or maybe next year?

Here are some actual promotion-related comments I've heard over the past few years, all by women who were either completely overlooked or did not get past the first interview:

- "How the F did he get promoted over me? I work twice as hard, and now I get to train him? This is an absolute shitshow!"

- "When I asked my boss what I need to do to become a Director, the only feedback he gives is 'you need more education.' I almost have my damn PhD and still haven't been promoted. How much more education do I need?"
- "My team went through a reorg and I'm grateful to still be here, but now I'm doing double the work. I asked about compensation and was told 'not this year'... really!"
- "I just completed my MBA and didn't even get an interview for the position I applied for. It was a promotion I had been waiting for. Why?!"
- "I've been at this company for more than 20 years. My leader knew my goal and knew that my perfect opportunity was posting, so why did the position post and not one soul reached out to me? By the time I noticed and reached out to the hiring manager, I had one day to apply. I asked if he could extend the posting and he said 'no, it was posted for seven days.' DUDE, I'm neck-deep in work that YOU need to have done. I would have expected a courtesy 'hey, we just want to make sure you were aware.' WTaF"
- "I made a mistake last year and I'm petrified that it's ruined my reputation. I'm afraid to do anything and it's killing me."

If any of these comments resonate with you, know that you're not alone. Many of the women I speak with can relate to at least one of these, often more.

Personal Journey to Empowerment

If you're reading this book, chances are you've been overlooked at promotion time even though you're working crazy hours, doing everything you can to get noticed, and constantly working in the trenches with your team. Perhaps you've forgotten the value you bring to those around you and to your organization. Maybe you've lost some confidence over the years. Perhaps you are nervous about putting yourself out there and taking a chance. Whatever is holding you back from achieving your next promotion, this book has you covered. My goal is that by the time you finish this book, you'll have gained confidence, started taking action, be back in the driver's seat of your career, and feel empowered to take big steps toward your next promotion or any other goal you have ahead of you.

My Journey: From Stuck to Soaring – Four Promotions in Ten Years

Before we go any further, let me share a bit about my corporate journey to help you understand why I relate so well to those of you struggling in this space. I didn't get into coaching the way many other career coaches do, with a ton of classes, studying, and coursework. See, I've actually walked in your beautiful shoes and, at one time, I was you... I was frustrated to no end and truly had expected that my boss was looking out for my best interest. It turns out that in some ways she was, but in others, not so much.

Early on in my leadership career, I spent ten years as a Project Manager. I led large technical projects for the California region of a giant telecommunications company. I knew I wanted to advance into a team leadership role but felt that I had to prove myself by working much harder than all of my peers. I needed to be "perfect."

During those ten years, to "prove myself", I took on more and more responsibility, leading three separate teams of people (yes, with a Project Manager title on my HR record), continuing to lead large technical projects, earning my Bachelor's degree, doing everything I could to make sure I was perfect and well-positioned for a promotion. I accepted my annual pay increases, which averaged 2-3% with a smile, and never asked for more. My leader knew that I had a goal of advancing my career, so it wasn't a secret. She also knew I got bored easily, so she would assign extra work to keep me happy. (Boy, was I naive.)

I worked my butt off, hoping, wishing, and praying that one day my boss would magically promote me. As you can guess, that didn't happen.

What actually happened is my boss took a new job and shortly afterward we went through a reorganization.

At that time, all of our jobs were posted with a slightly different structure, and we had to reapply for our next role or face a layoff. When I read the job descriptions of all the open roles, I realized that I was already doing more than the next level above me, which was a Billing Systems Manager role. So I decided to apply for that. After a few rounds of interviews, I was offered the job with a, hold your hats ladies, a whopping 4% pay increase. That was my first and biggest WTaF moment of my career. I felt like I was suddenly wide awake.

Much to the surprise of the hiring manager, I said, "Thanks, but no thanks," and walked out of his office. It was a huge "Hell no" moment for me!

Within ten minutes, I was invited into the office of the CFO. The CFO told me she was very surprised because she expected that I would be in that role, and they really didn't have a backup plan. She shared all the things that made me an asset to the company: my knowledge, success, strong vendor relationships, my team loved and respected me, and the fact that all of my cross-functional business partners trusted me and truly loved working with me. She asked me, "What will it take to make this offer more palatable to you?"

I thought for a moment and said, "I would like to have a Senior Manager title because I'm already exceeding the expectations of the Manager role, and I would like a 15%

pay increase." She said, "I assume you mean 15% on top of the 4% we already offered?" and (shaking my head no on the inside) I said, "Absolutely, thank you." She said, "Done." Now, full transparency, I had never negotiated for myself. I wish I had said 25% because that "ok" came really fast, but we'll tuck that lesson in for another time.

The day I was invited to the conversation with my CFO was the day I realized my true value to my team, my department, and my company. It was the day I made a promise to myself that I would never play small again. It was time to stop pursuing perfection and to become my own best advocate. It was a huge turning point for me as I shifted back into the driver's seat of my career. No more floating along, taking on a ton of extra work, and hoping that others had my best interest in mind.

I was very successful in the Senior Manager role, leading my team through projects that generated millions of dollars in revenue, improving processes, and most importantly, improving the skills of my team and elevating them. I was keeping track of my accomplishments and making sure that I maintained a high level of visibility. My confidence was at an all-time high!

Ten short months later, my team went through another reorganization. We were changing from a regional team structure to a division shared-services team structure. This meant we were consolidating seven regional teams under one organizational structure. All of our positions were being optimized, rewritten and reposted, and everyone in leadership roles had to reapply for their jobs or face layoffs. The Director positions were posted first. The plan was that once those roles were filled, the Directors would hire the Senior Managers, Managers, and Supervisors. There were seven Director roles being narrowed down to four. I decided to apply for a Director role. Remember, I had been playing small as a Project Manager for ten years, and I was ready.

As I started hearing from some of the Directors that they were being interviewed, I realized I had not yet been scheduled for an interview. I decided to reach out to the hiring manager, Lisa, and ask for a brief call, which she accepted. During the call, I let her know that I had heard some Directors were already interviewing and asked when my interview would be scheduled. She was very sweet and candidly told me they were trying to fit as many of the current Directors as possible into the four remaining roles. If they didn't fill all those roles with existing Directors, they would continue the search. She had been advised to only interview internal candidates with Director titles for those open roles. She then assured me I would have a management role on her team as she was well aware of my successes.

I thanked her for her honesty and asked permission to be candid with her. I shared my successes, with stats and metrics as proof. I shared that I had stayed in a role for ten years, which was about eight years longer than I should have as a Project Manager, and I shared what I had been doing as a Project Manager that was well beyond the job description. To say she was surprised would be an understatement. I told her I was ready for a Director role. I also shared I was ready to make a move. I was either moving up into a Director role, moving over to a new team to expand my knowledge, or moving out of the company completely. Within three days, I found myself on a flight to Denver, where I interviewed with seven Vice Presidents for the role of Director of Application Management. Less than a week later, I had a job offer in hand.

I was done playing small, and everyone knew it. I continued to advocate for myself, lead my team with trust and compassion, and maintain a high level of visibility with sponsors and business partners while building strong relationships. I took on more responsibility, made huge quantifiable impacts, including driving automation and saving 1000's of hours per year in manual labor and improving the quality of system coding to 98.99% from about 70%, and was promoted to Senior Director within a few short years. To this day Lisa still tells people I was her best hiring decision ever. Working under her was truly my favorite job of all time.

Then, as you can guess, several years later, in 2019, another reorganization came about. This time we were reorganizing from a division structure into a corporate/national structure, which meant that rather than leading people across seven states and three time zones, I would now be leading people across 40 states and four time zones. The plan of the corporate senior leaders was that the division leadership team would come into the new organization with their titles intact. The reality is this created inequity across teams as some people at my same level in the new organization had Vice President or Executive Director titles. My peers and I were expected to come across as Directors and Senior Directors. Um, no thank you!

I reached out to the head of the department and asked for a conversation. When we met, I let him know I was surprised we were not discussing titles and salaries. I shared my recent success and presented the additional responsibilities I was expected to manage. I stated that given everything I had just shared, I would expect a promotion to Executive Director, to level the field, and the appropriate pay compensation. He was surprised, to say the least.

The result of this conversation was that I was promoted to Executive Director and received a pay increase. My peers, who also had Director and Senior Director titles, were also promoted and financially compensated. The value of speaking up and opening the door truly made a difference for myself and others, who were mostly women. When we stop playing small, recognize our value, and articulate our worth clearly, we are a strong force and we set an example that elevates us and the women around us.

A few years later, in 2021, when I decided to leave my corporate career voluntarily after 27 years and 11 months, at the age of 50, in the middle of the pandemic, people were shocked. My boss literally choked on her water on the Team's call and all of my direct reports were in tears. I knew I had touched lives and made my impact. I also knew it was time for a change.

I heard comments from colleagues, friends, and family like: "But you've invested so much time," "Are you crazy?" and "But you make so much money"... and they were right (even a little about the crazy part). I had decided I was going to spend the rest of my working days helping women recognize their value, gain confidence telling their stories, and implement the strategies needed to succeed in reaching those big career advancement goals. I had enough "things," I had money in the bank, and I was ready to spend more time doing what I love.

Why Coaching: It Started with a Whisper

I always knew that I wanted to make a bigger impact, but I just didn't know how. In 2018, I attended a women's conference about "Leading with Power and Authenticity." The entire time I was there, I kept hearing this voice saying, "Why aren't you up there? Why aren't you leading this conference?" My imposter syndrome peaked as I compared myself to the ladies facilitating the conference. "They have PhDs", "They've worked with people all over the world"... you know all the usual BS our brains tell us. After the conference, the pull was strong. I hired a business coach to help me create a strategy, and I enrolled in a certification program. I launched my business on the side as "Tabatha Jones Consulting" and I coached anyone who would talk to me. I LOVED IT! So fast forward to 2021 when I left corporate and now 2024 where I just rebranded to...

Empowered Leadership Coaching™

Empowered Leadership Coaching™ is my coaching program where I help women like you achieve your career advancement goals faster by removing guesswork and frustration and providing the framework and strategies that can be implemented within your day jobs, without stress and overwhelm. These strategies are extremely effective. I have proven these strategies in my own career and in the careers of hundreds of individuals, mostly women—clients, colleagues, friends, and family. The most interesting part is that many of these strategies are so simple and obvious, you'll wonder why there isn't a career advancement handbook.

My program isn't your typical leadership training course where you make an investment, attend a few sessions, get a pretty certificate and don't implement anything. (I see you staring at your most recent certificate). Empowered Leadership Coaching is a holistic coaching program I created based on years of practice, implementation, and success. I've designed it to address all facets of leadership and personal growth, from boosting your confidence to enhancing your professional brand, and from setting strategic career goals to fostering a resilient and innovative mindset. In fact, this coaching program covers everything you need, all the way through interview and negotiation skills. This is a program loaded with learning, support, community, implementation, and so much strategy, which my clients have successfully proven works over and over again.

Some of my strategies will feel uncomfortable at first, but I encourage you to set perfection aside and experiment with them. Implementing these new strategies as you go through the program is the secret sauce to getting what you desire and deserve.

This program was born out of my personal journey and is tailored to help you achieve your career aspirations without feeling stuck for any longer than necessary. My mission is to guide you through a transformative experience that will empower you to take control of your career and never play small again.

Summary

In this chapter, we've debunked the myth that hard work alone is the key to career advancement. Instead, strategic work and self-advocacy are crucial. Through the Empowered Leadership Coaching Program, you'll learn the strategies that you need in order to recognize your value, articulate your worth, and take control of your career path. My journey from being overlooked to achieving four promotions in ten years is a testament to the power of these strategies. By embracing these principles, you can transform your career and achieve your advancement goals faster and with greater confidence.

By the end of this book, my hope is that you see the myths for what they are—myths. Embrace your power, take charge of your career! Now let's get started on your career journey and make magic happen.

Chapter 1 Reflection

Grab your journal and reflect on these questions:

- What myths or misconceptions have you encountered regarding women's career advancement, and how have they impacted you?
- How can embracing your power help you overcome these myths and advance your career?
- Identify a situation where you underestimated your own abilities. How can you reframe this experience to highlight your strengths?

"Confidence: Don't fake it until you make it, that's terrible advice. I want you to build it until you feel it." – Tabatha

CHAPTER 2

Overcome Obstacles with Unshakeable Confidence

Let's get real for a moment. We all face obstacles when it comes to achieving our career goals. Some obstacles are out of our control, but many are just stories we tell ourselves. It's time to rewrite your narrative and identify these obstacles so they don't continue to weigh you down and keep you frozen in place. Once these obstacles are removed, you'll also notice an immediate boost in your confidence.

Understanding Obstacles: Controllable vs. Uncontrollable

Uncontrollable Obstacles Uncontrollable obstacles are those you can't change. They may be frustrating, but they aren't always the end of the road.

Examples:

The position isn't open: Maybe the role you want isn't available right now, or there's a hiring freeze. Don't let this stop you—consider similar roles in different departments or other companies. Whatever you do, do not stop taking action.

- **Time and Title:** Some companies have strict policies about how long you need to be in a role before you can move up. Focus on elevating your leadership brand and preparing for when the opportunity arises. Don't wait idly; start taking steps now so you're ready when the time comes.

Controllable Obstacles When it comes to controllable obstacles, you have the power to change them. These often stem from imposter syndrome, self-limiting beliefs, misconceptions, assumptions, or false stories we tell ourselves.

Examples:

- **Self-disqualification:**
    - "I can't apply for that job because I don't meet all of the qualifications."
    - "I can't apply because I don't have a degree."
    - "I don't have enough experience."

  - "I know the person who does that job now; I could never do it like she does."
  - "I'm too old, no one will take me seriously."

- **Perfectionism or perfectionist paralysis:**
  - "I just need one more certificate, then I'll be ready."
  - "I just need one more skill before I can apply."
  - "I need to be in my job for 5 years before I'll be ready for the next role."

- **Fear of rejection:**
  - "The last time I applied, I didn't get the job; I can't go through it again."
  - "It's easier to just keep doing what I'm doing, rather than face rejection."

- **Imposter syndrome:**
  - "I can't do it as well as that person. She's so much smarter than I am."
  - "She looks so much more put together, and I'm a hot mess."
  - "I feel like I never have the answers."
  - "I'm just not good enough."

- **Not elevating as a leader:**
  - "I'm most comfortable working in the weeds with my team."
  - "My team calls me a micromanager, but I don't need someone else's mistakes making me look bad."
  - "I don't have time to think strategically."

- **Unclear on your value:**
  - "I can't even tell you what I do."
  - "I don't know how to explain what I do or why I am unique."

- **Not advocating for yourself:**
  - "I'm sure my boss has me covered."
  - "Someone will recognize my work and promote me someday."
  - "I don't want to be someone who brags about herself."

- **Too busy/no time:**
  - "My calendar is packed with calls; I can't focus on strategy."
  - "I don't have time to work on my goals, maybe once it slows down."
  - "I'm too busy to make time to meet with a coach or mentor."

- **Afraid to ask for guidance or support:**
    - "I don't want people to realize I don't know wtf I'm doing."
    - "Everyone else has figured it out; I'm sure I'll get there eventually."
    - "My boss is too busy to help me."

- **Stuck in the comfort zone:**
    - "I need to be the smartest person on my team, or I can't lead them."
    - "I'm working on this dashboard so it will be even easier for people to read the data."
    - "I'm just going to stay at my desk and work. They know where to find me."

- **Not recovering from past mistakes:**
    - "I don't want to take a chance; I made that one mistake last year, and I don't think anyone has forgotten it."
    - "That last mistake really changed another team leader's opinion of me. I don't want to put myself out there."

- **Fear of judgment:**
    - "I know that no one believes I'm ready."
    - "What if I go for it and fail? What will everyone think about me?"
    - "What if I make the wrong decision?"

- **Assumptions about what others think:**
    - "I'm pretty sure he thinks I'm not ready."
    - "My coworker wasn't hired, so I'm sure they think that no one on my team is qualified."

These behaviors are often self-sabotage, and you might not even realize you're doing it. It's time to get brutally honest with yourself and implement strategies to remove these obstacles ASAP.

Most controllable obstacles fall into three categories:

- **Time/Calendar Management:** Feeling like there's never enough time? It's time to prioritize yourself and your goals.
- **Mindset/Confidence:** Struggling to believe in yourself? Lacking confidence or knowledge? We can fix that.
- **Clarity:** Not clear on your value or what you should be focusing on at your level? Let's get you some clarity.

Overcoming Obstacles: Quick Wins in the First Month

Identify Your Obstacles: Be honest with yourself and pinpoint your personal obstacles. Are they controllable or uncontrollable? For the uncontrollable ones, think outside the box. Could another department or company be an option? For the controllable ones, it's game on.

Categorize the Controllable Obstacles: Break them down into Time, Mindset, or Clarity. (Some obstacles might overlap.)

Time/Calendar Management Obstacles: If your calendar is booked solid from dawn to dusk with no time for reflection, we need to talk. Many women think they're great at time management because they meet all their deadlines. But I challenge you to think differently because it means so much more. When do you work on your mindset, reflect on challenges, or focus on obstacle removal and problem-solving? When do you plan for your advancement?

In the Empowered Leadership Coaching Program, we tackle calendar management head-on. It's the key to success, confidence, and visibility. You need to block out time for you—your development, your brand building, your goals, and demonstrating your leadership. We'll talk more about this topic in the next chapter. For now, let's create a little "me-time."

Time Exercise: Create Some "Me Time"

- Review your calendar for the next two weeks.
- Find 30 minutes per week that you can use for reflection.
- Block out time for yourself and guard it fiercely.

Creating time for yourself will give you space to work on improving your mindset and clearing obstacles. Heck, when was the last time you set a little think time on your calendar? This isn't always intuitive, but it is a strategy of successful leaders. In one of our very first sessions, my client Carla said, "I've never thought about holding time on my calendar to just think." Those lightbulb moments are golden. I'm grateful that I get to witness so many of them.

Mindset/Confidence Obstacles: Now that we're clear on your time/calendar management obstacle, let's talk mindset. Journaling is a game-changer. It helps you identify whether the obstacles you're facing are real or just stories you're telling yourself.

Much of what's in your head is crushing your confidence. The "fake it until you make it" mantra? Nonsense. It's exhausting, and someone will always see through it. My confidence mantra is "don't fake it until you make it, build it until you feel it!" Let's clear those mindset blocks so you can shine.

Mindset Exercise: Journaling to Free Your Mind

- Grab your favorite journal tool—whether it's an app, a Google Doc, or a beautiful physical journal.

- Block 10 minutes every morning for journaling in a quiet, distraction-free space.
- Write down your mindset obstacles. For example:
    - "I can't apply for this promotion because I don't meet all the qualifications."
    - "I won't be promoted because the department head doesn't like me."
    - "I haven't done anything that matters, so no one will promote me."
    - "I'm not getting ahead because I don't have a degree."
    - "I'll never be as smart as my boss."
- Ask yourself: "Is this really true?" and "Can I prove it?"
- Then start writing. Write all the reasons that what you're telling yourself isn't true.

No one else will see this journal, so be honest and don't overthink it. If you can't get it all done in 10 minutes, set it aside and follow up on the thought tomorrow. There's no time limit, so give it the focus needed to clear it.

Often, you'll find that your limiting beliefs aren't true. Maybe someone's negative comment from years ago is still holding you back. Maybe a past mistake needs to be released. Maybe you're fixated on what someone else thinks about you. It's likely an assumption, so remember this: what others think about you is likely an assumption on your part and frankly, what other people think of you is none of your business. It's time to move forward.

Imposter syndrome and self-doubt can be tricky. Along with journaling, create a list of "50 Things You're Most Proud Of." Remind yourself of who you are and why you're so amazing. You're an unstoppable badass leader—and you deserve to start believing it.

Overcoming Perfectionism: Perfectionism can be a career killer. It held me in place for 10 long years. No one is perfect, and you are already exceptional in so many areas. If you're waiting until you meet 100% of the qualifications before applying for a promotion, it may come as a shock that your male counterparts are applying with only 60% of the qualifications and, guess what? They are getting hired and getting ahead. In fact, they are already following many of the strategies covered in this book because they never asked for permission or let themselves feel concerned about what others might be thinking or worried about making a mistake. When it comes to perfectionism, you have to realize that you're going to make mistakes—take the lesson and move forward. You're going to piss people off—apologize (if needed) and do what's right. Perfection is overrated.

Strategies to Overcome Perfectionism:

- **Self-Reflection and Documentation:** Regularly document your accomplishments, skills, and experiences. Reflect on your strengths and areas for improvement.
- **Building Confidence:** Create a list of achievements and review them often to boost your self-belief and confidence. I've actually encouraged clients to record the list and play it back when they feel themselves slipping. Give it a try!
- **Taking Risks:** If you see a job posting and it lights you up...***Apply for It***. Yes, even if you don't meet 100% of the qualifications. Focus on what you can bring to the role and how you can grow into it.

Clarity Obstacle: Not Clear About Your Value, Not Sure What You Should Be Focused On at Your Level: Clarity is key, but it often comes last in my framework because you need to create time to think, start removing obstacles, and rebuild a bit of confidence first. A lack of clarity can show up in several ways. Here are a few examples:

- **Not Having Clear Goals:** You have no idea where you want to go or what it will take to get there. Perhaps you know where you want to go but have no idea what it will take to land the role.

- **Not Knowing Your Unique Value or How to Measure Your Success:** When was the last time you thought about the value you bring to the business or to your team? Start by documenting your top five career accomplishments. Include stats and metrics—dollars, percentages, hours, ratings, etc. Set a monthly reminder to update your list.
- **Not Knowing What You Should Be Focused On at Your Level:** As a leader, you should be creating subject matter experts, not being the only one. Step out of your comfort zone and start showing up in new ways.

Remember, "What got you here won't get you there." The skills that got you into your current role aren't necessarily the ones that will help you continue to succeed and advance. Don't be afraid to ask for help.

Clarity Exercise: Get Clear on Your Value

- **Document Your Top 5 Career Accomplishments:** Start a spreadsheet or Google Doc.
- **Think About People and Projects Where You Have Made an Impact:** Include stats and metrics as much as possible.
- **Set Time on Your Calendar Every Month Going Forward and Add at Least One Additional**

Accomplishment: Keep your achievements current.

Quick Wins in the First Month To gain momentum early on, here are some quick wins you can achieve in the first month:

Time/Calendar Management:

- Identify and eliminate one non-essential meeting per week.
- Block out 30 minutes each week on your calendar for reflection.

Mindset and Confidence:

- Start a daily journal and commit to writing for 10 minutes every morning to clear obstacles.
- Create your list of "50 Things You're Most Proud Of."

Clarity:

- Complete the "Get Clear on Your Value" exercise.
- Have a candid conversation with a trusted colleague or mentor about your strengths and areas for development.
- If you're newer in your role and don't have clarity around expectations, ask for help. Don't wait until you're drowning.

By categorizing and addressing your personal obstacles, you can start turning them into opportunities. Time, mindset, and clarity are pivotal in this process. Implement these strategies, and you'll find yourself gaining confidence, taking action, and moving in the right direction.

Building resilience and managing setbacks is crucial. If you find yourself slipping into old habits, find a trusted friend or mentor to help you stay accountable. Don't let these obstacles control you—they can impact not just your career but your confidence and relationships outside of work. Taking these steps will lay a strong foundation for becoming promotion-ready.

Conclusion

Implementing these strategies and exercises will help you overcome obstacles, boost your confidence, and set you up for success. Continuously evaluate your progress, seek support when needed, and celebrate your achievements. Your journey to becoming a confident, promotion-ready leader starts now.

Summary

In this chapter, we've explored how to identify and overcome both controllable and uncontrollable obstacles. By focusing on calendar management, mindset, and clarity obstacles you can start making significant progress toward your career goals. The Empowered Leadership Coaching Program provides practical exercises, personalized support, and proven strategies to help you build unshakeable confidence and become promotion-ready. Embrace these tools, take action, and watch your career transform.

Chapter 2 Reflection:

- Identify Your Obstacles: What are the top three obstacles holding you back in your career? Are they controllable or uncontrollable?
- Time Management: How can you create more "me-time" in your calendar for reflection and personal development?
- Mindset Challenges: What self-limiting beliefs or negative thoughts are currently affecting your confidence? How can journaling help you overcome these?
- Clarity on Value: What are your top five career accomplishments, and how do they demonstrate your unique value to your organization?
- Overcoming Perfectionism: Think of a recent situation where perfectionism held you back. How can you adopt a more flexible and growth-oriented mindset moving forward?

"Progress over Perfection wins every time. If you want a promotion 6-12 months from now you need to start taking action now." – Tabatha

CHAPTER 3

Cultivate a Growth Mindset – The Key to Career Success

Let's talk about something that all of my successful clients have in common: they all have a strong growth mindset. Adopting this mindset is crucial for overcoming career obstacles and boosting your confidence. Plus, it's a lot more fun than staying stuck! Here's how a growth mindset can transform your professional journey and help you reach new heights.

The Magic of a Growth Mindset

Continuous Learning: Ever met someone who seems to always be on top of the latest trends and skills? They likely have a growth mindset. These individuals see every day as a new opportunity to learn something awesome. They're constantly improving, staying ahead in an ever-evolving work environment.

Resilience: Picture this: You hit a roadblock at work. Do you throw in the towel? Not if you have a growth mindset! You see challenges and setbacks as opportunities to grow. This resilience helps you bounce back stronger and stay motivated. It's like turning lemons into career-boosting lemonade.

Adaptability: In today's fast-paced world, adaptability is your superpower. A growth mindset makes you flexible and open to new situations, technologies, and approaches. Change doesn't scare you—it excites you! Being adaptable keeps you relevant and ready for anything.

Innovation: Want to be known as the idea person in your office? Embrace a growth mindset. It encourages creative thinking and innovative solutions, making you a valuable asset to any team. You're not just keeping up; you're leading the charge with fresh, exciting ideas.

Leadership: Leaders with a growth mindset are the kind of bosses everyone wants to work for. They inspire their teams to embrace learning and development, creating a culture of achievement and fun. As a leader, your growth mindset can turn your team into a powerhouse of innovation and success.

Career Advancement: Ready to climb the career ladder? Individuals with a growth mindset actively seek out and seize opportunities for advancement. They're not afraid to take on challenges that lead to personal and professional growth. With this mindset, you're always looking forward to the next big thing.

Increased Confidence: As you learn new skills and rack up achievements, your confidence naturally grows. A growth mindset reinforces the belief that you can tackle any obstacle and succeed. This newfound confidence is your ticket to articulating your value and grabbing those golden opportunities.

Focused Thinking: With a growth mindset, your thinking time becomes a powerful tool for progress. Instead of getting bogged down by negative thoughts, you focus on your goals and continuous learning. This positive focus drives you forward and keeps you motivated.

Growth Mindset and Self-Worth

Recognizing and embracing your unique worth becomes a whole lot easier with a growth mindset. It's like having a personal cheerleader who's always pushing you to be your best. Here's how embracing a growth mindset can boost your self-worth and impact:

- **Continuous Learning:** Commit to learning and skill development, knowing that every new skill adds to your value. It's like collecting awesome badges on your journey to career greatness.

- **Resilience:** View setbacks as learning opportunities rather than failures. This resilience will help you maintain confidence and stay motivated, even when the going gets tough.
- **Increased Confidence:** As you develop new skills and achieve more, your confidence will soar. This makes it easier to articulate your value and shine in your professional life.

Growth Mindset in Building Relationships

Building and leveraging a strong professional network is a whole lot easier with a growth mindset. This mindset encourages you to continuously seek learning opportunities, adapt to new situations, and stay resilient. Here's how it can improve your strategic relationships:

- **Continuous Learning:** Seek mentorship and guidance as opportunities for growth. Learning from others can give you new perspectives and insights that elevate your career journey.
- **Adaptability:** Be open to feedback and willing to adjust your strategies based on advice you receive. Flexibility in your approach strengthens your relationships and helps you grow.
- **Resilience:** Maintain and nurture relationships even when faced with setbacks. Use these

experiences as learning opportunities to build stronger, long-lasting connections.

Final Thoughts on Growth Mindset

Adopting a growth mindset is about embracing challenges, learning from setbacks, and continuously growing. It's the secret sauce to long-term success and fulfillment in your career and personal life. So, get ready to have some fun, embrace your growth mindset, and watch your career soar!

Summary

In this chapter, we've explored the transformative power of a growth mindset. By embracing continuous learning, resilience, adaptability, innovation, and leadership, you can elevate your career to new heights. The Empowered Leadership Coaching Program is designed to instill this growth mindset, providing you with the tools, strategies, and support needed to thrive in your professional journey. Embrace this mindset, and you'll see significant personal and professional growth, making you a confident and impactful leader.

Chapter 3 Reflection:

- How can you apply the principles of a growth mindset to your current career challenges?
- What steps will you take to cultivate a growth mindset in your daily professional life?
- Reflect on a recent setback. How can you view it through the lens of a growth mindset and learn from it?

"Setting boundaries to avoid burnout is a leadership skill. Set them with confidence."

– Tabatha

CHAPTER 4

Setting Boundaries and Managing Expectations

The Importance of Boundaries

One of the most critical skills for achieving career advancement is setting clear boundaries and managing expectations. Without boundaries, it's easy to become overwhelmed and burn out, making it difficult to perform at your best and showcase your leadership abilities.

Shortly after I was promoted to Director, I found myself feeling extremely overwhelmed. My leader seemed to be online working at all hours of the day and night, as was one of my new peers. This included replying to emails and instant messages during their vacations, early mornings, and late evenings. I was in my office with the door open, clearly looking very stressed, when my dear friend and colleague, Sandra, walked by. She came in and asked what was going on. I shared my dilemma, and that I may not have been ready to become a Director. She said these wise words to me, "You teach people what to expect. If you are always on, that becomes an expectation. Set your boundaries now." She added, "Even if you feel like working late at night or on vacation, save email responses and send them during business hours so you don't unintentionally create an expectation."

I reached out to my boss, Lisa, that day and had a heart-to-heart. She graciously explained that she didn't expect me to be on at all times; she was because that was her style and not an expectation she held for others. This conversation was a turning point for me, and I set clear boundaries for my work hours.

I established that while I would be flexible in emergencies, I would hold my boundaries on normal days. I made a habit of working a bit before starting my commute and checking email after my family was in bed. This allowed me to manage my workload effectively while still being present for my family.

Many women I've met are afraid to advance because of the "anticipated" expectations on top of their already busy lives. Take this lesson forward and hold your boundaries. You don't have to wait to advance your career just because you have a busy personal or family life. It's a choice you can make. Setting boundaries may feel a little uncomfortable at first, but will go a long way in setting you up for long-term success.

Strategies for Setting Boundaries

Communicate Clearly
Have an open conversation with your leader about your availability and boundaries.

Set Expectations Early
Establish your work hours and communicate them to your team and peers.

Model Healthy Behavior
Demonstrate a healthy work-life balance, encouraging others to respect their own boundaries.

Be Flexible but Firm
While being flexible in emergencies, ensure that you stick to your boundaries on normal days.

Chapter 4 Reflection Questions

- **Assessing Your Current Boundaries**:
  - Do you feel that your current work schedule allows for a healthy work-life balance?
  - How often do you find yourself working outside of your set hours?
- **Communicating Boundaries**:
  - Have you had a conversation with your leader about your work hours and availability?
  - How do you communicate your boundaries to your team and peers?
- **Maintaining Flexibility**:
  - In what situations do you find it necessary to be flexible with your boundaries?
  - How do you ensure that flexibility doesn't become the norm?
- **Creating and Sticking to Routines**:
  - What routines can you establish to help maintain your boundaries?
  - How do you plan to stick to these routines, even during busy times?

"Stop letting your calendar control you. You are a leader and that means you are expected to prioritize and say "no" as needed."

– Tabatha

CHAPTER 5

Elevate Your Career with Strategic Calendar Management

It may come as a shock to you, but 98% of the women I speak with are not strategic when it comes to calendar management. Sure, they get "all the things done on time," but are they getting "all the RIGHT things" done (or at least finding some balance)? When you're a leader aiming for a promotion, you need to be a pro at calendar management, using your time effectively to showcase your leadership abilities, presence, and poise. Calendar management can also lead to increased confidence, as you'll see in the transformations of my clients throughout this book.

Have you ever sat in a meeting and wondered how that amazing Director always has the perfect answer to questions you never even thought of? Do you marvel at how she always looks poised, confident, and in control? Her secret weapon is strategic calendar management—creating blocks of time to focus on what matters most. This sets her up for success, making her shine when it really counts.

Let's Assess Your Current Calendar

Take a peek at your own calendar. Do you have time blocked for "meeting preparation," "development," "team planning," "reflection," or "thinking/problem-solving"? How often are you multitasking in one meeting while preparing for another? Fun fact: this multitasking is killing your brand, making you appear disengaged in meetings you probably could have delegated, and underprepared in the meetings that matter—it shows, even if you think it doesn't.

Another fun fact (okay, not so fun): women often schedule a development opportunity or event (e.g., networking, lunch, hair appointment) on their calendar and then blow it off as soon as someone schedules a meeting. Ladies, at least 80% of the time it's perfectly fine to gracefully decline a meeting due to "another engagement" and ask the scheduler to find another time or accept a delegate.

Example 1: Michele's Lunch Dilemma

Just yesterday, I spoke with a very frustrated client, Michele. She works for a busy (chaotic) start-up, and her calendar is perpetually booked with meetings. She's frustrated because she has no prep time, so she's preparing during other meetings or working 15-hour days to catch up. She can't even take a lunch break because someone sees "lunch" on her calendar and overbooks it. This is not sustainable or healthy. When I asked what she does when someone overbooks her lunch, she said she attends the meeting and skips lunch. I advised her to set her lunch break to private immediately so people stop overbooking it because it's "just lunch." People will push your boundaries, and it's up to you to hold them. Emergencies and fire drills happen, but they shouldn't be the norm.

Example 2: Learning from Missed Opportunities

I attended a golf event last year hosted by a women's networking group. It was my first sponsored event since starting my coaching practice, and I was so excited. I'd never played golf and wasn't that interested in the game itself, but the networking opportunities were promising. Imagine my surprise (not really) when 85-90% of the attendees were men. When I asked the ladies who had confirmed they'd be there why they didn't show up, the unanimous response was "I had another meeting added to my calendar at the last minute." So weird, considering how many men made it work.

During that event, I witnessed new relationships being built, learned about hiring opportunities at my lunch table, and met countless people who are now in my network. I even won a trophy for the longest drive in the "women's" category. Yes, I'm still bragging about it. Yes, it's displayed in my office. And yes, it's because I didn't have much competition.

See ladies, it wasn't about golf at all. It was about an opportunity—a missed opportunity for many women who failed to see the bigger picture and recognize the opportunities to network, meet new people, build their brand, and learn about new career opportunities.

How many events have you missed because someone added a meeting to your calendar, overbooking your plans? How many times have you realized that the conversation could have waited or someone from your team could have been sent as a delegate? You do not have to attend every meeting that's added to your calendar. It's time to take control. And before you push back, I know that sometimes there are real fire drills, but every meeting is not a fire drill.

Calendar Management Assessment

Before diving deeper into strategies for effective calendar management, take this assessment to evaluate your current skills and identify areas for improvement.

Instructions: Rate each statement on a scale from 1 to 5, with 1 being "Strongly Disagree" and 5 being "Strongly

Agree." Be honest with your responses to get an accurate assessment of your calendar management skills.

- I regularly review my calendar to prioritize and plan my work week effectively.
    - (1) Strongly Disagree
    - (2) Disagree
    - (3) Neutral
    - (4) Agree
    - (5) Strongly Agree
- I allocate dedicated time for strategic thinking on my calendar.
    - (1) Strongly Disagree
    - (2) Disagree
    - (3) Neutral
    - (4) Agree
    - (5) Strongly Agree
- I create time to work on my career goals, development, and visibility every week.
    - (1) Strongly Disagree
    - (2) Disagree
    - (3) Neutral
    - (4) Agree
    - (5) Strongly Agree

- I create time on my calendar to prepare for employee 1:1s as well as my own 1:1s.
  - (1) Strongly Disagree
  - (2) Disagree
  - (3) Neutral
  - (4) Agree
  - (5) Strongly Agree
- I proactively block off time for breaks and self-care on my calendar.
  - (1) Strongly Disagree
  - (2) Disagree
  - (3) Neutral
  - (4) Agree
  - (5) Strongly Agree
- I am skilled at proactively managing and resolving scheduling conflicts (e.g., consolidation, delegation, elimination).
  - (1) Strongly Disagree
  - (2) Disagree
  - (3) Neutral
  - (4) Agree
  - (5) Strongly Agree
- I set firm boundaries and appropriately push back when someone attempts to overbook an event I have scheduled on my calendar.
  - (1) Strongly Disagree

  - (2) Disagree
  - (3) Neutral
  - (4) Agree
  - (5) Strongly Agree

- I have a system in place for setting and tracking long-term goals and deadlines on my calendar.
  - (1) Strongly Disagree
  - (2) Disagree
  - (3) Neutral
  - (4) Agree
  - (5) Strongly Agree

Scoring: Add up your scores for all the statements to determine your total score. The maximum possible score is 40. Interpret your score as follows:

- 8-16: Calendar Management Skills Need Significant Improvement
- 17-24: Some Strengths in Calendar Management, but Room for Growth
- 25-32: Good Calendar Management Skills; Continue to Refine
- 33-40: Excellent Calendar Management Skills; Keep Up the Great Work!

Client Story: Calendar Management is the Foundation

Every client who has successfully implemented my calendar management strategies has been pleasantly surprised. The most memorable recent conversation I had on the topic was with my client Carla's leader, Matt. During her program, Matt and I met monthly since her company had invested in her coaching. He shared feedback with me that he was seeing her confidence grow. He asked me what she was doing differently to get such a quick result. I shared with him that it all came down to calendar management. He seemed surprised. I explained that when we run from meeting to meeting, never allowing ourselves time to think, we can't possibly be confident or demonstrate our leadership abilities.

Carla had always felt under-prepared because she didn't have time set aside to prepare. By making space on her calendar, she now has time to consider her audience and intention, create effective presentations, and anticipate questions. This has led to her feeling more confident because she now knows that when she walks into a room she has her ducks in a row. I also explained that some people figure this out naturally, but for most women, it's not that easy, especially in a situation like Carla's where she was promoted into a higher-level leadership role and couldn't instinctively know what she should be doing differently or that she needed to elevate to become more strategic and less hands-on. Matt was clearly impressed with Carla's progress and recently approved for her to continue working with me.

Techniques for Managing Your Calendar Like a Next-Level Leader

Create White Space on Your Calendar. Delegate, Consolidate, Eliminate:

- **Delegate:** Identify meetings that can be handled by others, freeing up your time for more strategic activities. This also gives your team members an opportunity to demonstrate their abilities while building and nurturing trust.
- **Consolidate:** If you have multiple meetings on the same topic, reach out to the organizers and ask to consolidate.
- **Eliminate:** Remove meetings that are unnecessary. If there are already multiple people from your team representing you in the meeting, you probably don't need to be there too. If you aren't sure because a meeting invitation doesn't include an agenda or any helpful context, reach out to the organizer and ask for more details so you can make the best decision and spend your time wisely.

Create Time for Leadership Activities: (We'll go deeper into this area in future chapters.)

- **Prepare for Important Meetings:** 1:1s, presentations, etc. Think about your intention, audience, and message. Spend the time needed to make a great impression and stand out as a strong leader.

- **Get Visible:** Every Empowered Leadership Coaching client is required to go on a Visibility Quest. We'll dive into this a bit more in a future chapter, but I want you to start thinking about it as you're creating time on your calendar.
- **Networking and ERG Events:** Make time to attend and volunteer at networking events. This is a great opportunity to increase your visibility and demonstrate your leadership skills to people who may not normally interact with you.
- **Goal Setting, Problem Solving and Reflection:** These activities can help you stand out from a crowd of leaders as a poised, forward-thinking, and strategic leader.
- **Special Projects:**
    - **Stand Out:** Volunteer for high-visibility projects that showcase your skills and leadership potential.
    - **Strategic Initiatives:** Get involved in initiatives that align with organizational goals and provide exposure to senior leaders.

Prioritize Tasks that Align with Your Career Goals:

- **Focus on High-Impact Activities:** Identify tasks that directly contribute to your career advancement and prioritize them.
- **Set Clear Goals:** Ensure tasks aligned with your short-term and long-term career goals are on your calendar for some self-accountability.
- **Schedule Time for Your Development:** Courses, mentoring, or maybe the Empowered Leadership Coaching Program.

Scheduling Personal Time and Self-Care

In addition to professional activities, it's essential to schedule personal time and self-care activities into your calendar. Maintaining a balanced approach to calendar management ensures that you stay energized, focused, and resilient. Remember, you don't have to have a major vacation planned to schedule and enjoy PTO.

Here are some strategies:

- **Assertiveness:** It's okay to ask the scheduler to select a different time for appointments or meetings to ensure balance.
- **Self-Care:** Prioritize self-care to maintain energy and focus. Yes, a hair appointment is self-care, and you can get those roots done with a simple "I

have a conflicting appointment at that time. Can you please find a better time for this meeting?"

- **Exercise and Wellness:** Block time for physical activities like exercise, yoga, or meditation. These activities boost your physical and mental health.
- **Personal Interests:** Dedicate time to hobbies or activities that you enjoy. This can provide a much-needed break and refresh your mind.
- **Family and Friends:** Schedule regular time to connect with family and friends to maintain strong personal relationships and support networks.

Long-Term Planning

Be sure to add time into your calendar to work on your career goals. Take some time to map out the specifics of what you want to achieve, by when, and then add small deliverables onto your calendar so you can track your progress. Long-term planning involves setting both short-term and long-term goals and regularly reviewing and adjusting them. This practice not only keeps you focused but also ensures that you are continually moving toward your larger career aspirations.

Handling Unexpected Changes

The truth is that unexpected things will come up. Remember, I was an extremely busy executive at a fast-paced company myself, and no matter how much you plan for time for yourself, there are days when work issues will arise and get in the way. This is okay as long as you take the time to assess: Is this really an emergency or am I just reacting? It's also important to remember that just because the CFO has sent an email, that doesn't mean it's the most important part of your day. It's okay to ask: "When do you need this?" or to say, "I have a few things on my plate. Is it okay if I get back to you by Thursday?"

Quick Wins in the First Month

To help you gain momentum early in your journey, here are some quick wins you can achieve in the first month:

30-Day Calendar Management Challenge:

- **Week 1:** Identify and eliminate one non-essential meeting. If you are unsure or there's no agenda, reach out to the organizer to better understand the purpose.
- **Week 2:** Delegate two meetings to a team member. Schedule that time for networking, attending an ERG event, or development.
- **Week 3:** Consolidate similar meetings to increase efficiency. Hold the time you clear with "busy blocks."
- **Week 4:** Fill in "busy blocks" with important leadership activities, strategic thinking, and

preparation time. Reflect on your progress and adjust your plan as needed.

Weekly Goals and Check-Ins:

- **Track Progress:** Use a checklist or a planner to track your weekly goals.
- **Reflect and Adjust:** At the end of each week, reflect on what worked and what didn't.

Surprisingly to many of my clients, and I know you will find this as well, creating time for yourself on your calendar can help you clarify and move closer toward your goals, improve your mindset, and further develop your confidence.

Summary

Simple shifts in calendar management strategy can make a huge difference in how you're showing up for yourself, your team, your customers, and your senior leaders. By prioritizing, delegating, consolidating, and creating space, you can take control of your calendar and your career. Remember, the goal is to demonstrate your leadership abilities, presence, and poise effectively. These changes will not only help you manage your current role more efficiently but also position you as a promotion-ready leader in just three months.

“Stop letting your calendar control you. You are a leader and that means you are expected to prioritize and say "no" as needed.”

This chapter covers some of the strategies in the first module of the Empowered Leadership Coaching Program. By mastering calendar management, you lay the foundation for the next steps in your journey to becoming promotion-ready and advancing your career confidently.

Chapter 5 Reflection:

- How effectively are you currently managing your calendar, and what changes can you make to prioritize leadership activities?
- What are some specific meetings or tasks you can delegate, consolidate, or eliminate to create more time for strategic thinking?
- Reflect on how effective calendar management can boost your confidence and visibility. How can you implement this in your daily routine?

"Your value is not determined by others, but by your own ability to recognize your achievements and understand the impact you make."

- Tabatha

CHAPTER 6

Discover and Own Your Unique Value and Success

Ladies, you know we have a habit of downplaying our value and impact. I recently made a guest appearance on a podcast episode and talked about how we, as women, just get things done without pausing to reflect on the impact of our accomplishments. We almost never pause to recognize our success and celebrate.

I shared a fun example of this related to unloading a dishwasher, just to keep it simple:

Woman: Silently unloads the dishwasher and moves on to her next task.

Man: Loudly announces his accomplishment, detailing every step he took and the quantity of dishes he put away, then stands there proudly waiting for applause before moving on to his next task.

This humorous scenario highlights a serious issue: women often don't take the time to acknowledge our contributions or take credit for our work. We simply complete the task and move on, without recognizing the true impact or benefit of our success.

This habit can hold you back when it comes to career advancement. When writing a self-appraisal, meeting someone who can impact your career, or preparing for job interviews, you might struggle to recall and articulate your significant contributions. This can lead to missing out on the recognition or visibility you deserve.

Common Challenges in Recognizing Value

In my work with women preparing for interviews and career advancement, I've noticed two common tendencies:

- **Technical/Tactical Focus:** Many women dive straight into technical and tactical skills, neglecting to highlight the broader impact of their contributions and leadership success.
- **Team-Focused Language:** Always using "we" and "my team" instead of taking credit for your individual role in leading the team to success.

This doesn't help you stand out.

A few years ago, my friend Jackie asked me to review her resume. She wanted to apply for a promotion into a Director role. I glanced at it and immediately called her, asking if she was applying to be an Engineer or a Director of Engineering. She laughed because she immediately recognized her mistake. Her resume was all technical and tactical with zero reference to her leadership success. This indicated to me that during important conversations, she likely wasn't focusing on her success and was not establishing herself as the promotion-ready leader she was.

Another example comes from my former employee, Joyce. She was a very successful manager, and I knew she was ready for the next step on her career ladder. When she told me she had applied for a role in another department, I immediately contacted the hiring manager and let him know how amazing she was. After her interview, I reached out to ask him how it went, and the hiring manager told me, "She's nice and communicates well, but I have no idea what she can actually do for me. Her responses were all focused on 'my team' and 'we,' never once telling me what she could do. Unfortunately, I won't be moving her to the next round."

Holly's Story: From "I Don't Really Know What I Do" to "Yes, I Did Do That!"

One of my clients, Holly, came to me for coaching, and it became clear very early on that she struggled to understand her value. She could tell me what her team members could do and how amazing they were.

She could tell me success stats that they drove for the business, but she couldn't tell me anything that she specifically had done to inspire her team, drive success, and achieve business goals. After a bit of prodding and what I like to call a "fishing expedition" (we went really deep), we were able to break down her accomplishments. Holly was actually in awe as I read back to her the items I captured. We went from "I don't really know what I do" to "Yes, I did do that!"

Here's what we captured for just a few of her top accomplishments:

- **Orchestrated the workflow of over 3000 optical designs annually, totaling $200 million in value, to support global clients.** These designs represented a significant portion of total sales revenue within the product line, showcasing adept leadership, coordination of complex projects, and driving substantial revenue growth.
- **Devised and executed innovative workflow processes, slashing error rates to 2% per year or less from an initial rate of approximately 10%.** These improvements not only reduced errors but also enhanced functionality and reporting visibility. Additionally, she implemented a comprehensive project tracking system to ensure timely completion while preserving historical data integrity.

- **Enhanced efficiency and knowledge base across technical support groups by developing a structured curriculum for comprehensive cross-training programs conducted throughout the year.** These programs included training on pre-sales products, new architecture, and refresher courses to maintain sharp product knowledge and better support customers.
- **Spearheaded global training support procedures and scheduling workflows for over 40 engineers worldwide.** This optimized external training initiatives and streamlined processes, ensuring engineers received the necessary training to excel in their roles.

These stories illustrate, first of all, that Holly is a badass leader, and second of all, the importance of knowing your value and impact, especially as a leader who wants to advance. I see these issues often with my clients whether we're working on a resume and I need more information, preparing for a job interview, working on a year-end or quarterly self-evaluation, or preparing examples for a courageous conversation. Women want to include everyone and give everyone credit, it's part of what makes you a great leader, but…sometimes, sister, it has to be about you, and you need to find the balance if you want to advance.

Common Mistakes in Recognizing Value

- **Not Reflecting on the Impact of Your Work:** Set a calendar reminder to reflect for 30 minutes every week. This will help you pause and recognize the full impact of your work.
- **Undervaluing Your Accomplishments:** Don't dismiss your achievements as just part of your job. Acknowledge the impact and significance of your work.
- **Not Quantifying Your Value:** Without metrics or stats, it's hard to communicate your contributions effectively. Strengthen your achievements with data as proof, when possible.
- **Relying on Others to Speak for You:** While having advocates is important, take control of your narrative. Be ready to confidently communicate your value directly to those who need to hear it.

Overcoming Imposter Syndrome

Understanding and articulating your value often requires overcoming the obstacle of imposter syndrome. It's common to feel like you don't belong or aren't as capable as others perceive you to be. Consistently work on these feelings by:

- **Acknowledging Your Successes:** Regularly reflect on and document your achievements.
- **Seeking Feedback:** Honest feedback from trusted colleagues can help you see your strengths more clearly.
- **Building Confidence:** Practice discussing your accomplishments with friends or trusted colleagues until it feels natural.

Steps to Recognize Your Value

- **Reflect on Your Achievements:** Write down a list of things you've accomplished. Include actions that resulted in positive outcomes for your team or organization.
- **Add Metrics:** Quantify your impact with percentage improvements, cost savings, time reductions, employee satisfaction, or customer satisfaction scores. Consider hours saved, increased engagement, or improved morale.
- **Document Regularly:** Make it a habit to document your achievements. This prepares you for unexpected career conversations or opportunities and keeps you highly aware of your value.
- **Practice Articulating Your Achievements:** Practice discussing your achievements with

a trusted friend. This helps internalize your contributions and boosts your confidence.

- **Leadership Contributions:** As a leader, your team contributes significantly to your success. Understand how you drove the team forward, removed hurdles, closed gaps, managed vendors, engaged higher-level leadership, and collaborated with cross-functional departments. In a nutshell, this means be very clear on how you lead your team to success.
- **Mindset Matters:** Beware of letting your mindset play tricks on you. Recognizing your value and speaking about your accomplishments isn't boasting; it's essential for career growth. Don't let self-doubt diminish your confidence.

Interactive Exercises and Reflection Questions

Understanding Your Unique Value to the Business: If I were to ask you to tell me right now, what are your top 3-5 career accomplishments, could you answer? If I were to ask what is your unique value to the business, would you give me a confident answer or would I hear the crickets sing? This is a really big deal when it comes to career advancement because if you don't know your top accomplishments or your unique value, how can you successfully communicate it and how can anyone else know?

Challenge Yourself to Get Very Clear on Your Top 5 Career Accomplishments Think about anything you have done over the past 2-3 years that has helped drive your team or the business forward. As you are working on this, make sure you capture proof: stats/metrics about the accomplishment.

Write down anything you can think of without judgment, without overthinking, without wondering if it's cocky to take credit (it's not, so that's out of the way). Once you've created this draft, you can start formulating your top 5 by impact.

Examples:

- I spearheaded the development of an automated process that saves 50 hours of manual work per month.
- I identified and corrected a revenue leak that is now saving the company $80k per year.
- I implemented some process changes based on employee feedback that improved my employee survey scores by 2%.
- I recommended a solution that led to an improvement for our frontline agents, reducing call handling time by 1 minute per call.

Dig deep and remember that many of your actions have made a positive impact and you need to give yourself credit.

What Counts as a Metric? Anything that quantifies your accomplishment. Not everything will have a numeric metric and that's okay. Just make sure you lay it out clearly. Start digging for this data now—look at past reviews, SLA data, dashboards, and other data sources or reports that show KPIs that you impact.

Create a Skills Inventory What are your top skills? What are you known for? Soft skills matter and don't forget your leadership skills.

Unique Value Statement After you take some time to think about your accomplishments and skills—you're going to have a more clear picture of your Unique Value.

- How do you stand out from your colleagues?
- What are you better at than anyone else?
- What sets you apart from your competition?
- How do you know these are true?

Write down the things that make you unique and why this makes you an asset to the business. For example:

When reflecting on my own corporate career, one example of my unique value was my multifaceted perspective. I could see things from the frontline, customer, and technical viewpoints, which allowed me to drive decisions effectively. My background in Customer Care, where I started by answering phones in a call center, combined with my experience leading technical teams of coders and automation creators, gave me an edge that many others in technical leadership roles did not have.

In the coaching world, where there are thousands of career coaches, one example of my unique value is my extensive hands-on experience. I worked as a ladder-climbing corporate executive for more than 20 years and successfully led and coached technical leaders and teams while navigating my own career growth. My blueprint wasn't created from hours upon hours of sitting in a theory-based classroom, but from real-world experience and achievements.

For my client Susan, her unique value lies in her ability to methodically approach situations from multiple perspectives: customer experience, financial, and operational. She can then tell a story using meaningful data that the senior leadership team can use to drive progress and make informed decisions.

For my client Carla, her unique value is her talent for building authentic relationships. These relationships benefit her company's fundraising efforts, support the foster youth her organization serves, and enhance her own growth and development. I'm in awe every time she shares the name of a new person she has met and nurtured a relationship with. These connections are often powerful women who further contribute to her success as a Director of Development and as an individual.

Identifying your unique value can be challenging so create time and space to think about it. If you are really struggling, ask a mentor, your leader, or business partners. It's okay to ask for help.

The most amazing part of this process is that, once you've taken these actions, you'll feel your confidence start to elevate.

Now, you may be thinking, how can I use this information?

You can use it to update your resume, LinkedIn, and internal applications. You can use it to prepare stories that you can use in interviews and you can use it as you're gaining visibility or networking, which we'll cover in future chapters.

Summary

Understanding your unique value is crucial for career advancement. If you don't track your accomplishments and learn to articulate them, no one else will be able to and it will slow you down. By regularly reflecting on and documenting your achievements, you'll boost your confidence and be prepared for new opportunities. Embrace your unique value and let it shine through in every professional interaction. This practice will help you in your current role and make you a strong candidate for promotions and new opportunities.

"Your value is not determined by others, but by the recognition of your own achievements and the impact you make."

Chapter 6 Reflection:

- Identify Your Impact: What are your top five career accomplishments? Describe how each one has positively impacted your team or organization. What specific metrics or outcomes can you use to demonstrate this impact?
- Overcome Imposter Syndrome: Think about a recent situation where you felt imposter syndrome. How did this feeling affect your performance or mindset? What specific achievements or feedback can you focus on to reinforce your self-worth and combat these feelings in the future?
- Seek Constructive Feedback: Who can provide you with honest, constructive feedback on your strengths and areas for improvement? How can you use this feedback to better understand and communicate your unique value?
- Leverage Your Skills: Which of your skills have been most crucial to your career success so far? How can you further develop these skills to enhance your professional growth and leadership capabilities?

"Don't give anyone else control of your career advancement. You need to get in the driver's seat."

– Tabatha

CHAPTER 7

Claim Your Spotlight – How to Effectively Share Your Achievements

Alright, ladies, it's time to shine! You've been documenting your successes, defining your unique value and building your confidence. Now, let's make sure the world knows about it. While chatting with your boss, friends, or peers about your achievements may be comfortable, it's crucial to extend these conversations to leaders outside of your immediate circle. Believe me, these leaders are the ones who can drop your name into those rooms where promotion opportunities are discussed. And yes, these conversations really do occur and they occur more often than you think.

Ever hear a disappointed woman say she didn't get a promotion and doesn't know why? Often, it's because she hasn't communicated her unique value and success with enough impact during networking, conversations, and job interviews. Let's change that!

But Isn't It Cocky to Talk About My Accomplishments?

I'm asked this question a lot: "Isn't it cocky to talk about my accomplishments?" My answer is always, "No! The goal is to be confident." Trust me, your male colleagues never worry about sounding cocky. In fact, the fact that you're reading this book tells me that you are 100% not cocky, so own your success, sister!

Preparing for Courageous Conversations

To effectively communicate your value, preparation is key. Here are some essential steps:

- **Be Clear on Your Achievements:** Know your accomplishments and experience well enough to answer questions quickly and confidently.
- **Know Your Unique Value:** Get very clear on your unique value and get comfortable talking about it. How do you stand out from others? What is something you do better or differently?
- **Create a Compelling Personal Elevator Pitch:** Think about who you are, what you have done, and your areas of expertise. Highlight an accomplishment you are particularly proud

of, share your goals, and be ready to ask for what you need (e.g., sponsorship, mentorship, introductions, or feedback).

My Journey to Confidently Articulating My Value

Putting myself back into the driver's seat of my career and learning how to confidently articulate my value secured me three of my four promotions! After my promotion to Senior Manager and a serious mindset and confidence shift, I was back in control of my career. No longer hoping my boss had my best interests in mind, I intentionally and confidently kept my own career advancement goals top of mind!

Once I learned to track my successes and get comfortable talking about my accomplishments, advocating for myself became a breeze. Ten months after my promotion to Senior Manager, we went through another reorganization. Seven directors had to reapply for four positions, and I, confident Senior Manager, applied as well. When I didn't initially get called for an interview, I reached out to the hiring manager.

In that conversation, I was prepared to discuss my accomplishments and share my work experience that was not represented in my HR records. For example, I led a team of nearly 400 vendors, project owners, and stakeholders through the largest billing system conversion in the company's history. I had stellar employee survey scores and, after conducting some gap analysis, I was able to elevate my newest team's skills significantly over the past 10 months. I had a lot of metrics to back up my success, but won't bore you with them. I also shared that I wasn't planning to apply for a lateral role after a very successful ten years of doing Senior Manager or higher-level work with a Project Manager title.

After clearly articulating this information, I found myself on a flight to Denver, where I interviewed with seven Vice Presidents. I was able to clearly articulate the exact job I was applying for (leading a very technical team) and explained why I was the best candidate without even being asked why. (This is one of my secret interview strategies)

Sidebar: Often, when women interview for technical leadership roles, they miss the very important leadership aspect and go straight to their technical expertise. I've also met women who have missed out on opportunities because their imposter syndrome tells them they can't apply for a role leading a technical team. They forget that their leadership skills are the most important skills when they want to advance into leadership roles. I spoke at the WICT Network Tech It Out Conference a few years ago and wish you could have seen the women's faces light up when I said, "Leadership is not a technical skill. (Ask me how I know this is a fact.)

Anyway, very soon after this interview, I had a job offer in hand. Later promotions were easier because I tracked and consistently communicated my achievements to my leader, to her leader, and to others who needed to know.

In 2019, as we transitioned to a corporate structure, I realized that in the new organization my peers would have higher titles despite my increased responsibilities. I was assured this would be assessed in the future, which was not the right answer. I requested a conversation with the department head, shared my accomplishments, and discussed the reasons why I deserved a higher title and pay increase based on my new scope. This led to my promotion to Executive Director, aligning my title and pay with my responsibilities. It also led to the promotion of several others who were in the same boat but were not as confident in asking for what they deserved.

In this case, being able to articulate my unique value allowed me to hold the door open for other women who may not have been as clear or confident.

Crafting Your Elevator Pitch

Once you are clear on your unique value and feeling like you're ready to showcase it, you need to craft a strong elevator pitch. Your elevator pitch should summarize your areas of expertise and your unique value proposition in a concise, impactful statement. It should be clear, specific, and tailored to your audience. As you work to tailor your elevator pitch, think about what you might want to ask for when networking and meeting leaders in your organization.

Practice delivering your pitch until it feels natural.

Examples of Elevator Pitches:

- **General Networking:** "Hi, I'm [Your Name]. In my role as [Your Position], I've led [Project/Initiative], which resulted in [Metric/Outcome]. I'm passionate about [Industry/Field] and am currently looking to [Your Goal]. Would you be willing to [Your Ask]?"
- **Job Interviews:** "My name is [Your Name], and I have [Number] years of experience in [Field/Industry]. My areas of expertise include [Skills]. The accomplishment I am most proud of is [Accomplishment], which led to [Outcome]. I'm eager to [Your Goal] and would love to discuss how I can contribute to [Company/Department]."

Applying Your Value Proposition in Different Contexts

Once you have completed your pitch, identify opportunities to integrate it into conversations. This can include general networking conversations, informational interviews, job interviews, and introductions to new people.

Contextual Examples:

- **Networking Events:** Use your pitch when meeting new people at industry events or other professional groups. Your ask may be for more introductions, discussing opportunities, etc.
- **Informational Interviews:** Tailor your pitch to highlight your skills, experience and unique value. Remember to ask for what you need from each person you interview.
- **Job Interviews:** Adapt your pitch to answer the common question, "Tell me about yourself," focusing on your most relevant achievements and skills.
- **Everyday Introductions:** Be prepared to use a shorter version of your pitch in casual settings, such as an introduction in an actual elevator, or in passing, to a new leader at your company.

Common Mistakes to Avoid

- **Undervaluing Your Accomplishments:** Many women think, "It needed to be done, so I did it," without considering the impact of their achievements. Always recognize the value of your contributions. Avoid using "we" too much and take credit using "I." It's a balancing act, so practice.

- **Not Quantifying Your Value:** Make sure to quantify your impact with metrics or examples to demonstrate your contributions clearly.
- **Relying Solely on Others to Advocate for You:** While having supporters is beneficial, take control of your narrative and communicate your value directly.

Key Tips

- **Always Be Ready to Advocate for Yourself:** Reflect on your accomplishments and be ready to share them. You never know when you'll run into someone new or someone who can help bring your name into the rooms that matter. This will also help you with building confidence, which will help you in future job interviews. .
- **Build Your Confidence:** Practice talking about your accomplishments and other successes until it flows naturally. It will be awkward at first, but it gets easier.
- **Be a Champion in Helping Other Women:** Share this book and your learnings with other women to help them build confidence. We have to work together to change the statistics and help women get the recognition they deserve.

Preparing for Important Conversations

When promotion opportunities arise, you want your name to come up positively and from multiple people. Make sure leaders know your value and contributions, so you aren't just a name without context.

Chapter 6 Challenge: Take the 10-Day Elevator Pitch Challenge

- **Day 1-3:** Draft your elevator pitch. Focus on who you are, your key achievements, areas of expertise, and what you want to achieve.
- **Day 4-6:** Refine your pitch. Ensure it's concise, compelling, and reflects your unique value.
- **Day 7-10:** Practice your pitch with a trusted colleague or mentor. Get feedback and make necessary adjustments

Additional Practical Exercises

- **Record Yourself:** Record your elevator pitch on your phone. Playback to check for clarity, confidence, and conciseness. Make adjustments as needed.
- **Peer Review:** Pair up with a colleague for a mock networking event. Practice delivering your elevator pitches to each other and provide constructive feedback.

- **Continuous Improvement:** Set a monthly reminder to review and update your elevator pitch based on recent achievements and feedback.

Client Story: Kelly's Journey to Advocate for Her Worth

I met Kelly at a stand-up paddleboarding event. When she learned that I'm a Career Advancement and Leadership Coach, she asked if we could connect soon to talk about her work situation. Kelly, a highly skilled Project Coordinator, found herself in a familiar situation. She excelled at her job, loved her company, and respected her boss, yet her title and pay didn't match her responsibilities. Her duties were equivalent to those of a Project Manager, yet she was earning less and held less authority. This misalignment led to frustration and self-doubt.

Kelly's case represents a common challenge faced by women. Despite performing at a higher level, they struggle to advocate for themselves and secure the recognition they deserve. Like me, in my early career years, they eventually wake up and wonder what the heck is happening and how so much time has passed.

We dove into Kelly's goals and discussed her desire to stay with her current company. She loved the people she worked with, her schedule, and the work itself. The challenge was clear: She needed to initiate a conversation that would align her title and pay with her responsibilities. We worked closely to identify her daily responsibilities, quantifiable achievements, and the positive impact she had on the business. We used steps from the Empowered Leadership Coaching program framework to prepare her to confidently ask for what she deserved. Role-playing conversations helped bolster her confidence.

Shortly after our last session, Kelly initiated the courageous conversation with her boss. She presented her case (supported by data) and outlined her accomplishments and the value (supported by facts and metrics) she brought to the organization. It paid off as she emerged with the title of Operations Project Manager and a substantial pay raise!

Today, Kelly is thriving, doing the work she loves with a team she values. Her journey exemplifies the power of self-advocacy. As I always say, "You can't be told 'yes' if you don't ask." Just think about it, if Kelly hadn't asked, it's highly likely that nothing would have changed.

Your journey begins with a single step...and you're the only one who can take it. Oh! If you're waiting for your boss to simply promote you, refer back to my story and save yourself the frustration and 10 long years.

Summary

Understanding and articulating your value with confidence is crucial for career advancement. By consistently communicating your achievements and maintaining a compelling elevator pitch, you ensure that your contributions are recognized and appreciated. This practice not only positions you as an invaluable asset to your organization but also makes you a strong candidate for promotions and new opportunities.

Articulate Your Value and Stand Out

One of the core elements of the Empowered Leadership Coaching Program is teaching you to articulate your value confidently. The "10-Day Elevator Pitch Challenge" is designed to help you craft, refine, and practice a compelling personal elevator pitch. By the end of this challenge, you'll be ready to present your value to anyone, anywhere.

Understanding your value and being able to communicate it effectively is not just about self-promotion; it's about ensuring that your contributions are recognized and appreciated. This proactive approach sets the stage for your career growth. Embrace your unique value, articulate it with confidence, and let it pave the way for your career advancement.

Chapter 7 Reflection

- What specific achievements can you highlight to demonstrate your leadership abilities?
- How can you practice discussing your accomplishments to build confidence in articulating your value? Who can you practice with?
- Reflect on a recent conversation with a supervisor or colleague. How could you have better communicated your value and contributions?

"If you want to be viewed as a promotion-ready leader, you must start presenting yourself as promotion-ready now. Don't wait until the position posts. It's much harder to try to prove yourself in a job interview than it is to already be standing out as the obvious choice."

– Tabatha

CHAPTER 8

Stand Out and Shine: Elevate Your Career Through Visibility

Sarah applied for her dream promotion and didn't even get called for an interview. She was shocked because it was a role she believed she was well-positioned to succeed in. When she requested a conversation with the hiring manager, he told her, "No one on the panel knows you. In fact, one person said, 'I don't see her as a leader of this team; all I've ever seen her do is present data in meetings.'" Now, I know Sarah personally. She has done a lot of amazing things, and she's an exceptional leader, but if I hadn't worked directly with her, I wouldn't know either. She worked hard but wasn't investing time and effort into building her brand and boosting her visibility.

Dani reached out to me via LinkedIn feeling defeated. She had completed her MBA and was so proud of her achievement, but she was devastated when she didn't get the promotion she interviewed for. Again, no one knew what she was capable of. She was so focused on being the best technically and education-wise that she neglected her visibility for several years and forgot to highlight her leadership skills during her interview, which was very clear during our conversation.

These are just a few stories that illustrate the fact that working hard and striving for perfection is not the solution. I've met so many women exhausted, frustrated, and frankly pissed off because they are literally working themselves into the ground, burning the candle at both ends, taking class after class, and never getting promoted. Friends, you have to focus on the bigger picture—it is not all about who's working the hardest.

It's also the reason that so many of the women I speak with are now training their leader, who was promoted instead of them. I often hear, "It's office politics," or "He barely does anything, so WTF?" or my favorite, "It's because that person has a degree and I don't." Though some of these may be true *sometimes*, most of the issue honestly comes down to a lack of visibility.

While you've been working hard, checking all the boxes, becoming more "perfect," and working in the trenches with your team, that person was having conversations, talking about their success, and making sure that their name was on the minds of the people who could impact their career advancement.

I want you to really lean in here because this is going to be uncomfortable, but it will make a difference in your career that you can't even imagine right now.

The Importance of Visibility

When it comes to career advancement, people in your company need to know who you are. There are plenty of ways to make sure this happens, but most likely, you aren't taking advantage of any of them. You are working hard, keeping your head down, and staying in your comfort zone. This is not helping you elevate and demonstrate your leadership, build your brand, or prepare for the next step on your career path. It is definitely not helping you stand out as the "obvious candidate" before your dream job posts.

Building and Maintaining a Strong Professional Presence

Building and maintaining a strong professional presence while expanding your network and increasing visibility is how you can ensure that your name comes up in those important promotion conversations.

It's imperative that those who have influence know you, understand your goals and contributions, and that they have an opportunity to see you in action, demonstrating your leadership consistently - during the good times, the challenging times, and the day-to-day.

Questions to Ask Yourself

- How are you proactively making the time to get in front of senior leaders and showing up as someone with strong professional brand?
- When you have an opportunity to show up as a strategic, innovative forward-thinking leader, are you?
- Do you often miss visibility opportunities because you're "just so busy"?
- When a senior leader introduces herself to you, are you seizing the opportunity to introduce yourself beyond your name, department, and job title?

If you think your professional presence may not be strong enough, ask yourself this question: If Tabatha were to reach out to five senior leaders in my company, what would they say about me? If you don't know, we have work to do, my friend.

Visibility Quest

As I shared earlier in this book, I send my Empowered Leadership Coaching clients on a Visibility Quest. Use some of the white space you've created on your calendar to pencil these activities in.

Conduct Informational Interviews

One powerful way to boost your visibility is by conducting informational interviews with leaders at your company, especially those who hire for the roles you want. These interviews can provide valuable insight into what is needed for advancement and help you build relationships with decision-makers.

As you prepare for informational interviews, you need to be very intentional:

- **Who do you need to meet with?**
  - Consider leaders who are in the roles you aspire to reach.
  - Consider leaders who hire for the roles you aspire to reach.
  - Consider other influential leaders in your organization.
    - Make sure there is a balance of diversity so you get different perspectives when possible.

- **What do you want to know from each person?**
    - Create a short list of questions that will help you achieve the outcome you desire from each conversation. You can ask any work-appropriate questions, but here are a few examples:
        - What advice do you wish someone had given you earlier in your career?
        - Who are your mentors and what value do they add to your career?
        - What core strengths do you look for when hiring leaders on your team?
        - Can you recommend two people in this company that I should connect with as I continue my leadership development and pursuit of my next promotion?

There are more Information Interview questions in the Tools and Resources section at the end of this book to help you prepare.

Sponsoring or Taking Leadership Roles in ERGs

ERGs are a great way to learn about other cultures and people. They are also a way to become more visible and build your brand with people who may not interact with you in your day-to-day role. If you're at a level that can sponsor ERGs or join the board, do it! It's another way to increase your exposure and experience while serving others.

Practical Steps to Enhance Your Visibility

- **Public Speaking:**
    - Internal Presentations: Offer to present at team meetings or company-wide events.
- **Professional Networks:**
    - Join Industry Groups: Become active in professional organizations.
    - Attend Networking Events: Make it a point to attend at least one networking event per month.
- **Informational Interviews:**
    - Reach Out: Reach out to leaders within and outside your organization for insights and guidance.
- **Special Projects:**
    - Volunteer for High-Visibility Projects: Showcase your skills and leadership potential.

- Get Involved in Strategic Initiatives: Align with organizational goals and gain exposure to senior leaders.

Networking Strategies

Building and Maintaining Relationships: It's important to maintain and nurture relationships. Often, we get "busy" and neglect our relationships outside of our immediate team or project scope. This can really hurt when it comes to career advancement. Don't wait until you need help to start building relationships. It's much easier when people already have a connection to you and already know, like, and trust you.

Make a conscious effort to check in with colleagues, mentors, and professional contacts regularly. This can be as simple as a quick email or text, a coffee chat, or a LinkedIn message.

Leveraging LinkedIn: LinkedIn is a great place to meet new people and build relationships. Connect authentically with people in roles or industries that interest you.

Engage with posts, share insightful content, and participate in discussions relevant to your field. This not only increases your visibility but also positions you as a thought leader.

Meet for a virtual coffee break and be openly curious. Most people want to help you, but so don't worry about "bothering people" or assume they don't have time for you. That's not true; this is you getting in your own way again.

Attend virtual events. You'll meet a variety of people with common interests. Be sure to connect and follow up.

Do's and Don'ts for Networking Events

Do's:

- **Do Prepare:** Have a clear idea of what you want to achieve from the event. Prepare your elevator pitch and key talking points.
- **Do Be Genuine and Curious:** Approach conversations with authenticity and genuine interest in others.
- **Do Follow Up:** After meeting someone, send a follow-up email or LinkedIn message to reinforce the connection.
- **Do Listen More Than You Talk:** Show genuine interest in others by listening attentively and asking thoughtful questions.
- **Do Share Contact Information:** Ensure you have business cards or digital means to share your contact information easily. (iPhone tap and the LinkedIn scan are excellent digital options.)

Don'ts:

- **Don't Be Pushy:** Networking is about building relationships. It's not about making immediate gains. Avoid aggressive self-promotion.
- **Don't Monopolize Conversations:** Give others the chance to speak and engage with different people.
- **Don't Neglect Body Language:** Maintain positive body language. Smile, make eye contact, and avoid crossing your arms.
- **Don't Forget to Take Notes:** If you have meaningful conversations, jot down some notes afterward to help you remember key details.
- **Don't Wait Until You Need Something:** Build and maintain your network consistently, not just when you need a favor.
- **Don't Forget to Follow Up:** Set a follow up plan and stick to it. Simply setting a calendar reminder can help with this.

Visibility Tips for Introverted or Quieter Personalities

If you identify as an introvert or have a quieter personality, networking and increasing visibility might feel especially daunting. Here's a strategy to make this easier: find yourself a confident wing-woman. Having someone who is more talkative join you at networking events can help bring you into conversations and introduce you to others. These wing-women are usually great at talking to everyone and can provide the support you need to engage more comfortably. I know this works because I often serve as the wing-woman for my quieter colleagues and friends.

30-Day Visibility Boost Plan

Week 1:

- Identify and sign up for one networking event or ERG meeting.
- Reach out to a leader in your organization for an informational interview.

Week 2:

- Volunteer to present at the next team meeting or company-wide event.

Week 3:

- Attend the networking event or ERG meeting and actively participate.
- Follow up with the leader you interviewed, thanking them and summarizing what you learned.

Week 4:

- Schedule another informational interview with a different leader.
- Reflect on your progress, adjust your strategies, and set goals for the next month.

Summary

Visibility is crucial for your career advancement. By building and maintaining a strong professional presence, conducting informational interviews, and following practical networking strategies, you can ensure that your name is top-of-mind during important promotion discussions. Remember, it's not just about working hard—it's about making sure your hard work is recognized by those who can help you advance.

Chapter 8 Reflection:

- How can you increase your visibility within your organization and industry?
- What steps can you take to build and enhance your professional brand?
- Reflect on a recent networking opportunity. How did you present yourself, and what could you improve?

"Surround yourself with those who can see your potential even when you can't. Mentors, sponsors, and coaches are your career accelerators."

– Tabatha

CHAPTER 9

Build Your Dream Team – Finding the Perfect Mentors, Sponsors, and Coaches

Building and leveraging a strong professional network, or your "advisory board," is crucial for career advancement. This network should include mentors, sponsors, and coaches—the no-nonsense folks who will give you the unvarnished truth, even when it stings a little. Understanding and cultivating these relationships is key to climbing the career ladder faster and more successfully.

The Difference Between Mentors, Sponsors, and Coaches

Understanding the distinct roles of mentors, sponsors, and coaches is essential. Each plays a unique part in your career growth:

- **Mentors:** These wise individuals provide guidance, share knowledge, and offer advice based on their experience. They're often a few steps ahead of you in the company. Think of them as your personal career GPS—helping you navigate your path, avoid potholes, and get you back on track when you hit a dead end.
- **Sponsors:** These champions actively advocate for you, opening doors to new opportunities and promoting your achievements. They're the higher-ups who say, "Have you heard what she did?" at key meetings. They're your career megaphones, amplifying your achievements to the decision-makers.
- **Coaches:** Focus on developing your skills, improving performance, overcoming obstacles, and setting/achieving goals. As a coach, I'll help you identify and implement strategies to become a more successful leader and get positioned for advancement. Coaches are your personal trainers—holding you accountable, cheering you on, and sometimes telling you to drop and give them 20 (metaphorically, of course).

Identifying and Cultivating Relationships

Building these relationships requires a strategic approach. Here's how to identify and cultivate relationships with mentors, sponsors, and coaches.

Mentor and Sponsor Identification Week

To quickly identify and approach potential mentors and sponsors, dedicate a week to this task:

Identify Potential Mentors and Sponsors

- **Mentors:** Make a list of individuals with experience in your field who have achieved what you aspire to. They should be approachable, willing to share their knowledge, and preferably 1-2 steps ahead of you.
- **Sponsors:** List leaders within your organization or industry who have the influence to advocate for you. They should be familiar with your work and potential. If they aren't yet, these are the perfect people to add to your "Visibility Quest."

Research and Prepare

Understand their backgrounds, accomplishments, and current roles. This will help you tailor your approach and make a strong first impression.

Reach Out

Write a simple email to initiate contact. Be clear about your intentions and how you believe they can help you. Here are a few conversation starters:

- "I'm currently working on building my professional network and would love to secure a few mentors and sponsors. Would you be open to a conversation as I believe you may be the perfect (mentor, sponsor, coach) for me?"
- "I've been following your work on [specific project/initiative] and would love to learn more about your experience and insights."
- "Can you share some of the key challenges you faced in your career and how you overcame them?"
- "What advice do you wish someone had given you earlier in your career?"

The Role of Mentors, Sponsors, and Coaches in Career Advancement

Mentors, sponsors, and coaches each play a critical role in helping you advance your career. Remember, you own the relationship. This means it's your responsibility to set up each meeting, create the agenda, and arrive prepared. Don't make the mistake of wasting their time, or they will stop investing in you.

Here's a tale of two mentees from my past to illustrate my point:

Mentee #1: Charmon: Charmon was a star. She regularly scheduled calls with me, sent her questions in advance, and arrived at each session ready to drive the conversation. Her preparation meant our meetings were productive, and she left with clear advice and action items. Charmon implemented the strategies we discussed, and within 12 months, she secured two promotions—from Sr. Manager to Director to Senior Director. Her success was a direct result of her commitment, preparedness, and willingness to take uncomfortable action based on the advice I gave her.

Mentee #2: Liz: Liz was the flip side of the coin. She often forgot to schedule follow-up meetings or allowed other things to overbook our time. (Refer to calendar management chapter), didn't send agenda items or questions without prompting, and showed up without a plan or intention. Her lack of prioritization and follow-through meant our sessions were unfocused. After six months, I had to have the "it's not me, it's you" talk and told her to reach out when she was ready to truly invest time in herself.

A mentor, sponsor, or coach can't do the work for you. All of the coaching and mentoring in the world won't help if you don't take action.

To help you experience the most success possible, here are practical steps to cultivate these relationships:

- **Regular Check-Ins:** Schedule regular meetings to update them on your progress and seek their advice.
- **Be Intentional with the time:** This person is also busy and is taking the time to invest in you.
- **Show Appreciation:** Always express gratitude for their time and support. Acknowledge their contributions to your growth.
- **Be Proactive:** Take the initiative in maintaining the relationship. Share your achievements and challenges, and ask for their insights on specific issues. Create and send an agenda in advance so your mentor has time to prepare.

30-Day Relationship Building Plan

Week 1:

- Identify and list potential mentors, sponsors, and coaches.
- Research their backgrounds and current roles.

Week 2:

- Draft personalized emails and reach out to at least three potential mentors and sponsors.

- Schedule introductory meetings or informational interviews.

Week 3:

- Follow up with those who responded positively.
- Prepare for your meetings by listing key points and questions.

Week 4:

- Conduct your meetings and gather insights.
- Reflect on the advice received and adjust your strategies.
- Send thank-you notes expressing your gratitude and outlining your next steps.

Summary

Cultivating strategic relationships with mentors, sponsors, and coaches is essential for career advancement. By understanding their distinct roles and actively seeking out these relationships, you can build a strong "advisory board" that supports your growth. Use the "Mentor and Sponsor Identification Week" to kickstart this process, and leverage the provided tools and strategies to maintain and strengthen these connections.

Chapter 9 Reflection:

- Who are potential mentors, sponsors, and coaches within your network, and how can you approach them?
- What is your intention for each relationship: Mentor, Sponsor, Coach?
- Reflect on a current professional relationship. How can you strengthen it to support your career advancement?

"You can't control when your next promotion opportunity will post, but you can control your readiness ***BEFORE*** *it posts."*

– Tabatha

CHAPTER 10

Acing Your Promotion Interview – Prepare for Interviews Early

Don't wait until the job posting for your dream opportunity goes live to start working on your interview preparation. Many promotions require a complete job interview, and many women make the mistake of believing they are a "shoo-in," only to get into the interview and fail. They fail because they underestimate what it takes to prepare, they don't take the time to identify leadership-level successes and prepare impactful stories that highlight their achievements, experience, and skills, and they undersell themselves in interviews because "everyone on the panel knows what I've done."

Spoiler Alert! When there's a panel interview, the panel is required to compare candidates objectively and decide on the candidate who is the best fit for the role. You can't tell half of your story (or less), expecting someone else to piece it together and move you forward. That wouldn't even be a fair and equitable hiring practice. Save yourself the tears, frustration, and embarrassment by investing time in this now.

Client Story: Danielle Interview from Embarrassed to Ecstatic!

Let's talk about my client Danielle. She was the top salesperson at her food brokerage company, a huge achievement, especially for a woman. Bright and fun, Danielle was so excited when her dream job at a large food distributor was posted. During the interview, she failed miserably. She was referred to me shortly afterward by an acquaintance I had met at a winery (an example of the power of visibility and networking. Yes, I practice what I preach). When we met for our consultation, Danielle was in tears, embarrassed by her interview performance. She knew she needed help and, though concerned initially about the investment, she decided to move forward with my one on one coaching program.

We started working together, diving deep into her experience and success. About six weeks later, her dream job was reposted. She asked if she could reapply, and I told her, "HELL YES YOU CAN!" Nervous but determined, she applied again. This time, she not only made it through multiple rounds of interviews, but the Vice President asked her what was different because she had done so much better and displayed so much more confidence. She shared that she had hired a coach (me) to help her build confidence, understand her value, and tell her story. There are some secret strategies that I share with clients and Danielle implemented them like a champ, but being able to tell her story with so much impact and confidence made a huge difference in her success.

She landed the job, and we then negotiated a much higher salary (which in 1 year alone was nearly a 5x ROI on her coaching program investment). This highlights the importance of building confidence, understanding your value, and preparing for interviews well before the job posts. Interviews are hard, and you have to be strategic in order to stand out. You can't wait to start working on this strategy until the job is posted, or you may not have the best experience.

Preparing for your next promotion opportunity requires strategic planning and consistent effort. By dedicating time to update your resume, document your stories, and practice interviewing, you can ensure that you will be ready to seize any opportunity that comes your way.

90-Day Promotion Prep Plan

To help you stay on track and make meaningful progress, here is a 90-day plan to elevate your resume, position your experience examples into powerful stories, and improve your interview readiness.

Month 1: Update Your Resume and Create Interview Examples

Week 1:

- **Set Weekly Goals:** Dedicate specific times each week on your calendar to work on these tasks.
- **Resume Review:** Start by reviewing your resume. Focus on updating your experience and accomplishments, including relevant stats and metrics. Use your "50 Things I'm Most Proud Of" and Unique Value documents to gather some of this information.
- **Simplicity is Key:** Use a simple format and don't bury your details in long paragraphs.

Week 2:

- **Leadership Focus:** Ensure your resume highlights your leadership skills, experience, and relevant accomplishments that demonstrate your abilities and success as a leader. I don't think I can say "leader" many more times here, but you are a leader and your leadership strength and success need to be clear. Leadership, leadership, leadership.

- **Metrics Matter:** Include quantifiable achievements such as percentage improvements, cost savings, time reductions, revenue increases, and team successes.

Week 3 & Week 4:

- **Document Interview Examples:**
    - **For Job Specific Examples:** Use my simple hack: Grab a similar job posting and copy it. Go into ChatGPT and type: "Based on this job posting, what questions should I be prepared to answer during a job interview (paste job posting)." Enter.
    - **For Behavioral Interview Questions:** Most leadership-level interviews will include behavioral questions. Make sure you incorporate some of these into your documentation.
        - Tell me about a time when you failed to deliver on a promise.
        - Tell me about a time when you made a mistake.
        - Tell me about a time when you demonstrated successful leadership.

    - Tell me about a time when you had to deliver a difficult message.
    - Tell me about a time when you experienced a conflict with your leader or coworker.

- **Strengths and Weaknesses:** Be prepared to talk about both.
- **Write Your Examples Into Impactful Stories:** Think about your experience and accomplishments and how you can bring them into your interview by telling impactful stories. Use SPECIFIC examples rather than broad ones. This will set you up for the most success and best highlight your experience.
- **Use the STAR Format:** Structure your responses using the STAR format to provide clear, concise, and impactful answers.
    - **Specific Situation:** Describe the specific situation/example within which you performed a task or faced a challenge at work.
    - **Task:** Explain the actual task or challenge that was involved.
    - **Action:** Detail the specific actions you took to address the task or challenge.

        - **Result:** Share the outcomes or results of your actions, using quantifiable metrics where possible.
    - Even if the experience was negative, find the positive result and tell the story. This is especially helpful when sharing a failure or a missed deadline example.

Month 2: Practice Interview Skills

Week 1:

- **Identify People Who Can Practice with You:** People who actually interview others are excellent choices. Request time with these individuals so you can practice. Set the time on your calendar.

Week 2:

- **Mock Interviews:** Schedule mock interviews with trusted colleagues or mentors. Record these sessions to review your performance and identify areas for improvement. Avoid overusing "we" or "my team"; focus on your individual contributions and leadership impact.

Week 3:

- **Reflect on Feedback:** Think about the feedback you were given after each mock interview. Listen to the recordings. Identify your mistakes and work to improve.

Week 4:

- **Refine Answers:** Based on feedback from mock interviews, refine your answers and practice them until you can deliver them confidently and naturally.

Month 3: Interview-Related Activities

Week 1:

- **Enhance Your Skills:** Identify any skill gaps that may hinder your promotion and seek out training or professional development (coaching with me) opportunities.

Week 2:

- **Industry Research:** Capture updates on industry trends, department projects/goals, and company news. Being well-informed demonstrates your commitment and strategic thinking. This will help you stand out even more.

Week 3:

- **Networking:** Reach out to your professional network for insights and advice. Networking can provide valuable information about the promotion process and potential opportunities.

Week 4:

- **Final Preparations:** Review your resume, practice your stories, and ensure you are mentally and physically prepared for the interview. Confidence is key!

Key Additional Points Many people miss out on great opportunities because they underestimate what it takes to prepare for an interview.

I offer interview prep-only packages and include this in all of my programs, because it's critical to your success when it comes to career advancement and in most cases it takes a minimum of 4 hours of time with me, plus about 10-20 hours on your own. So you can see why you don't want to wait until the job posts to start thinking about this.

The Most Common Mistakes in Interview Prep:

- Waiting until the job posts to start preparing

- Not being articulate: Rambling or not answering the whole question
- Not telling the whole story using a SPECIFIC example
- Not sharing the outcome using data when possible
- Assuming that the panel knows you so you don't have to respond completely

Avoid These Mistakes By:

- **Documenting Stories of Your Experience:** Start preparing examples as soon as you know you want to advance. You can grab some common behavioral interview questions from Google and think about what's going to be important to the role you're applying to.
- **Having a Catalog of Examples:** Having a variety of experience examples to pull from is helpful because you never really know what will be asked. The STAR method is the most popular: Specific, Task, Action, Result.
- **Strengths and Weaknesses:** Be ready! Talk about an honest strength and weakness and how that strength has benefitted your team in the past and how you've worked to overcome the weakness and hold yourself accountable.

If you start working on this now, you will realize how much think-time this takes and why it's almost impossible to prepare in just a few hours.

Summary Promotion preparation is an ongoing process that requires strategic planning and consistent effort. By following the 90-day plan, you will ensure that you are ready for promotion opportunities within three months. Updating your resume, preparing powerful stories, and practicing interview skills will position you as a confident and capable candidate, ready to advance your career.

The Empowered Leadership Coaching Group Program includes an entire component focused on resumes and interview preparation. The amount of time this takes is often underestimated. Also, the timing of when a job posts is out of your control, so my clients remain in the program for 12 months, allowing you to stay fresh and ready for interviews as well as receive coaching advice as you receive feedback or progress. Through structured exercises, personalized coaching, and continuous support, the program prepares you to seize promotion opportunities confidently and effectively. By integrating these strategies into your daily routine, you will continuously build your professional brand and position yourself for ongoing career growth and success.

Chapter 10 Reflection:

- What are your key strengths and accomplishments that you want to highlight in an interview?
- How can you use the STAR format to prepare compelling stories for your interviews?
- Reflect on a past interview experience. What went well, and what could you improve for next time?

"Rejection is redirection. Embrace setbacks as opportunities to learn, grow, and come back stronger."

– Tabatha

CHAPTER 11

Harness the Power of Resilience

So, you've done all the right things, implemented all of my strategies, and still didn't get the promotion you expected. It happens. Maybe someone had a bit more experience, or perhaps there's a major change coming that you're not privy to yet. Whatever the reason, it's crucial not to throw in the towel, speak negatively to others, or revert to old habits. Take a moment to recover, then get back on that horse. Resilience matters!

Strategies to Handle Setbacks

1. **Celebrate Your Growth**
    - You took a risk and did some truly courageous things. Reflect on what you've learned and how you've grown through the

process. Seriously, celebrate your growth and the hard work that got you here!

2. **Look for the Lesson**
   - Analyze the experience to understand what you can learn from it. Identify areas for improvement.
3. **Seek Constructive Feedback**
   - Ask for feedback. Listen with an open mind, thank the person, and follow up if you have questions. Consider asking for their support as you work towards improvement.
4. **Consider Coaching**
   - Determine if coaching could be a good fit for you. If so, ask your leader to support you. Many companies consider coaching an educational expense.
5. **Stay Resilient and Visible**
   - Don't give up! Keep going and stay visible. Maintain your network and stay engaged.

Practical Tips for Moving Forward

1. **Reflect and Journal**
    - Spend time journaling about your feelings and the situation. Writing helps process emotions constructively and gain clarity.
2. **Set New Goals**
    - Use the setback as a catalyst to set new, achievable goals. This keeps you forward-focused and motivated.
3. **Maintain a Positive Mindset**
    - Reframe your thoughts to see setbacks as opportunities for growth. Positive self-talk and affirmations are powerful tools.

Client Story: Susan's Journey

Remember Susan from an earlier chapter? She went from "I could never fill my boss's shoes" to "I've outgrown my job, I'm ready for a promotion." After a reorganization in the telecom industry, her boss left, and Susan had the chance to apply for her boss's job. Despite being the most qualified candidate in her department and doing all the right things, she didn't get the promotion. The feedback was positive, but they chose another candidate with a very different background, indicating likely changes in the role's focus. A few months later, another reorganization occurred, and Susan applied for a Division Senior Manager role, which she landed. By being ready and staying positive and resilient through a setback, Susan's brand remained strong, showcasing even more of her amazing qualities.

My Own Story

When I was a PM, my Director took another role. I believed I was the most qualified candidate to replace her, even though it was a title leap. But in a team meeting, we learned that another Director would absorb our team. I was shocked and, if we're being honest I was beyond pissed off. I went home and took a sick day to process my disappointment. It was better to take time off than to say something I'd regret.

The first reorg eventually led to my promotion to Sr. Billing Systems Manager, which also led to me recognizing my true value to the company for the first time. Shortly after, I learned that another reorg was coming. Had I been promoted earlier, I would have been at higher risk of layoff. Instead, I used what I learned about myself and through my experience to land a Director role just 10 months later.

Inspirational Quote: Rejection is Redirection

After not landing a job several interviews in, my job-seeking client, Rachel, told me, "Rejection is just God's redirection." It's so true. Though it may not feel good at the time and you can't possibly know the future, it often is a good thing in the long run.

Developing Resilience

1. **Building Emotional Intelligence**
    - Understand and manage your emotions. Recognize how your feelings impact your thoughts and behavior. This self-awareness is crucial in developing resilience. Avoid negative comments that could backfire and hinder your future advancement.
2. **Mindfulness and Stress Management**
    - Practice mindfulness techniques such as journaling and deep breathing to manage stress and stay focused. Integrate these practices into your daily routine.
3. **Seek Support**
    - Reach out to mentors, colleagues, and friends for support and advice. Sharing your experience can provide new perspectives and encouragement. If setbacks are significantly affecting your ability to move forward, consider seeking help from a coach, like me, who can prevent you from overthinking, hurting your brand or getting stuck.

4. **Continuous Improvement**
    - Identify areas for improvement and seek out training or educational opportunities to enhance your skills. Stay adaptable and open to new opportunities; sometimes, the path to success involves taking unexpected detours.

Summary

Handling setbacks effectively is crucial for long-term career success. By celebrating your growth, seeking feedback, staying resilient, and continuously improving, you can turn setbacks into stepping stones for future achievements. Remember, setbacks are not the end of your journey but rather an integral part of your growth and development. Embrace them, learn from them, and keep moving forward. The Empowered Leadership Coaching Program is here to support you every step of the way, providing you with the tools, strategies, and community you need to thrive in your career. Together, we can turn setbacks into setups for success.

Chapter 11 Reflection

- How have you handled past setbacks in your career, and what did you learn from them?
- What are some ways you can celebrate your growth to help you move forward after a setback?
- Reflect on a recent setback. How can you leverage your resilience and resources to bounce back stronger?

"Hiring a coach and asking for help isn't a sign of weakness; it's a strategic power move. The right coach will help you unlock your potential and accelerate your career growth."

– Tabatha

CHAPTER 12

Leverage Coaching – Why and How to Choose the Right Career Coach

Choosing the right career coach can be a game-changer in your professional journey. With a coach, you gain personalized guidance, accountability, and an objective perspective on your career development. In the Empowered Leadership Coaching Group Program, you also gain strategies that you can implement immediately. You are part of a community of like-minded, goal-focused, and supportive women in the safe space we've curated for you.

Here's how to effectively find and choose a career coach, along with real-life success stories to illustrate the impact of coaching.

The Benefits of Hiring a Career Coach

- **Personalized Guidance:** A career coach can provide tailored advice and strategies that align with your specific goals, strengths, and challenges. It's like having a GPS for your career path, minus the "recalculating" voice.
- **Accountability:** Coaches can help you stay on track by setting goals and deadlines, ensuring you maintain momentum and focus. Think of them as your personal cheerleader who doesn't let you hit the snooze button on your dreams.
- **Unbiased Feedback:** Coaches can offer objective insights into your performance, helping you identify areas for improvement and celebrate your successes. No sugar-coating here, just the sweet truth!
- **Skill Development:** Whether it's enhancing your leadership skills, improving your communication, or learning to negotiate, coaches can provide the tools and support you need.
- **Networking Opportunities:** Coaches often have extensive networks and can introduce you to influential contacts in your industry.
- **Eliminating Imposter Syndrome:** Coaches can help you recognize and overcome feelings of self-doubt and inadequacy, showing you that you truly belong and deserve your success.

- **Building Confidence:** Through continuous support and positive reinforcement, coaches can empower you to believe in your abilities and take bold steps towards your goals. Imagine having a confidence boost on tap!

Growth Mindset and Career Coaching

A growth mindset is essential for maximizing the benefits of career coaching. By embracing this mindset, you can fully engage in the coaching process, continuously seek improvement, and remain resilient in the face of challenges. Here's how a growth mindset can enhance your coaching experience:

- **Continuous Learning:** Use coaching as an opportunity to develop new skills and knowledge.
- **Resilience:** View coaching feedback as a tool for growth. Use it to improve and stay motivated.
- **Adaptability:** Be willing to adapt your strategies and approaches based on the insights gained from your coach. Flexibility isn't just for yoga.

How to Find and Choose a Career Coach

- **Identify Your Needs:** Determine what you want to achieve with a coach. Are you looking for help with leadership skills, job search strategies, or work-life balance? Knowing what you need helps you when it comes to hiring the right coach.

- **Research and Recommendations:** Ask for recommendations from colleagues, mentors, and professional networks. Use online platforms like LinkedIn to find coaches with strong endorsements.
- **Check Success Records:** Look for coaches with a proven track record of success. It's not always about the letters after their names. Ask for references and/or check LinkedIn Recommendations.
- **Schedule Consultations:** Meet with potential coaches to discuss your goals, ask questions, and gauge if their coaching style aligns with your needs. It's like a first date, but without the awkward silences. Beware of the high-pressure sales tactics that are sometimes used in the coaching world. You decide when you are ready.
- **Evaluate Fit:** Choose a coach you feel comfortable with and who demonstrates a genuine interest in your success. Trust and rapport are crucial for an effective coaching relationship. Think of it as finding your professional BFF.

Sample Questions to Ask Potential Coaches

- **Do you personally coach or are there a lot of recorded learning modules?** Many coaching programs rely on recorded modules and self-paced curriculum. This doesn't work for everyone, especially busy female leaders.

- Empowered Leadership Coaching clients are coached via live calls every week. Recorded modules are available in case you miss a call or want to review a session in the future.

- **Can you describe your coaching process and outcomes?** Knowing your needs and their promised outcomes will help you determine whether you're fully aligned. Some coaches are more focused on mindset, some weave in spiritual work (woo-woo), and some are more like me—focused on strategy and tactical approaches with a balance of mindset.
    - Empowered Leadership Coaching clients learn and implement strategies to ensure that they elevate as leaders, develop their teams, and stand out as promotion-ready in all the right ways. We build success habits and implement them as we go.
- **What types of clients have experienced the most success in your program?** Programs are geared for different clients with a variety of needs. Make sure this answer aligns well with who you are and what you're seeking.

    - The clients who have experienced the most success in the Empowered Leadership Coaching program are Managers and Directors who are ready to stop struggling and simplify career advancement and leadership growth. This is not a program for clients who are looking for a band-aid fast fix. We all know those things don't lead to lasting habits and successful outcomes.

- **Do you offer Group or One on One Coaching?** Both have benefits and each serves a different purpose. Group coaching should be very personalized and structured to meet the goals of the clients. One on One is much more customized and free flowing.

    - In the Empowered Leadership Coaching Group Program we have a supportive community of goal-focused, like minded individuals adding to perspective and insight.
    - Our One on One Empowered Leadership Coaching Program is best for someone with very specific concerns who is looking for more specialized support.

Client Story: Carla's Story – A Case Study in Coaching Success

Carla, a Director at a nonprofit organization, reached out to me after hearing a podcast episode where I discussed imposter syndrome and its impact on Gen-X women. Promoted from Manager to Director in 2020, Carla was struggling with the transition. She felt like an imposter, unconfident, and full of self-doubt. Despite her hard work, she just wasn't sure of how to change things. We've done a lot of work together, but here are a few highlights:

Step 1: Clarifying Roles and Responsibilities We began by discussing the differences between her former Manager role and her new Director role, focusing on the need for a more strategic and forward-thinking approach. Carla started implementing these strategies immediately, elevating her presence as a powerful Director.

Step 2: Strategic Calendar Management We created white space in her calendar by delegating, consolidating, and eliminating time-wasting meetings. This allowed her to focus on critical leadership activities—visibility, planning, thinking, and leading. Carla quickly saw the benefits as she gained confidence and started showing up feeling more prepared during critical meetings.

Step 3: Managing Up We worked on strategies for "managing up" to get what she needed from her leader. This included several exercises and strategies, including owning her own 1:1 agenda and driving it, rather than simply following her leader's agenda. By demonstrating her ability to be proactive and goal-focused, Carla improved her interactions with her leader. Her leader, who also received some coaching when he met with me (shhh, he doesn't know), was thrilled with Carla's growth.

Step 4: Engaging Her Team Carla implemented new strategies within her team to become more engaged and inspiring. By adding structure to her employee 1:1s and prioritizing her team's development, she received positive feedback from her direct reports. She also made a few shifts in the strategy of her team meetings to freshen them up and make them more engaging. She received rave reviews. This boosted her confidence and solidified her leadership role. Her direct reports were frequently commenting that they could see the difference in her confidence and leadership since she had been working with me.

Step 5: Increasing Visibility and Networking We prioritized networking to showcase her confidence and build her professional brand. Carla achieved one of her 2023 goals early and was invited to a VIP event full of high-powered female leaders. She confidently navigated the event with a strong elevator pitch and proactive planning. No more playing small and feeling "less than." She was starting conversations, sharing her elevator pitch, and following up. Her superpower has always been relationship building, but now that is even more elevated!

Outcome: Carla's confidence and overall leadership improved significantly as a result of our work together. She was brave, took fast, uncomfortable action, and implemented new strategies nearly every week, building new habits that are keeping her confidence high. She's now preparing for a powerful year-end performance conversation with her leader and has created a strategic advancement plan for herself and her team's future. Her story highlights the transformative impact of investing in leadership growth and seeking help when needed.

Client Story: Holly's Journey to Recognizing Her Unique Value

Holly, a Director in the telecommunications industry, reached out to me for coaching and it became clear very early on that she struggled to understand her value. She wanted to advance her career and had been considering a transition to a company that better aligns with her values, but felt very stuck and unclear on how to move forward.

Here's how we worked together to transform her career:

Step 1: Identifying Goals We started by identifying Holly's career goals. Achieving a few of her goals would eliminate a big chunk of her imposter syndrome.

Step 2: Creating a List of 50 Things I'm Most Proud Of To help Holly recognize her value as a whole human, I asked her to create a list of 50 things she was most proud of in her career and her life. This exercise was challenging but incredibly eye-opening. As we went through the list, Holly began to see the breadth and depth of her contributions, which are so much broader than her job.

Step 3: Deep Diving into Strategies We dove into strategies to free up time on her calendar, engage more with her team, and build her brand. By delegating tasks and eliminating time-wasting meetings, Holly created white space in her calendar to focus on high-impact activities.

Step 4: Focusing on Identifying Her Unique Value Through our sessions, we broke down her accomplishments and clarified her unique value at work. Holly was in awe as I read back to her the items I captured. We went from "I don't really know what I do" to "Yes, I did do that!"

Step 5: Increasing Visibility and Networking Holly began attending networking events and sharing her compelling elevator pitch. This increased her visibility and helped her build valuable connections in her industry.

Step 6: Making Power-Move Decisions Together, we are now working to figure out the specific "next steps" of her career. It's always a power move when you make the decision rather than letting someone else make it for you. Now that Holly knows she's a valuable catch for any company, it's time to narrow down - "should I stay or should I go now?" (It's okay to sing it).

Outcome: Holly's mindset, clarity, and overall leadership have improved as a result of our work together. She has been brave and implemented new strategies. She is focused on elevating her team and now also includes time on her calendar to focus on elevating herself. Her story highlights the transformative impact of being vulnerable, asking for help, and investing in yourself.

These stories illustrate that my clients are badass women who know what they want. They are not afraid to invest in themselves and will work hard to achieve the outcomes they deserve.

Crafting an Action Plan with Your Coach

Once you've chosen a coach, collaborate to create a personalized action plan. This plan should include:

- **Clear Goals:** Define short-term and long-term objectives. Think of them as your career's GPS coordinates.
- **Specific Strategies:** Outline the steps and actions needed to achieve your goals. Roadmap to success, anyone?
- **Milestones and Deadlines:** Set realistic timelines to monitor your progress. Because what's a plan without a timeline?
- **Regular Check-ins:** Schedule consistent meetings to review your progress, adjust your

plan, and stay accountable. Consistency is key, like your morning coffee.

By asking for help and incorporating a growth mindset, you can make significant strides in your career advancement. Embrace the support, guidance, and insights that a Career Advancement and Leadership coach, who has walked in your beautiful shoes can provide, and watch as your professional journey transforms in powerful and unexpected ways.

Chapter 12 Reflection:

- What specific goals do you want to achieve with the help of a career coach?
    - Consider both short-term and long-term objectives that you would like to accomplish.
- How can a growth mindset enhance your coaching experience and outcomes?
    - Reflect on how embracing continuous learning, resilience, and adaptability can improve your professional development.
- Reflect on a time when you received valuable feedback or guidance. How did it impact your career, and how can coaching provide similar benefits?
    - Think about the specific ways feedback has helped you grow in the past and how a coach can offer similar or even greater support.

"Your journey toward career advancement is a continuous process of growth, learning, and adaptation."

– Tabatha

CHAPTER 13

Transform into Promotion-Ready – Next Steps with Empowered Leadership Coaching

As we wrap up this journey toward your career advancement, it's important to revisit the steps that will help you become promotion-ready within three months. By now, you have a clear understanding of some of the strategies and tools necessary to navigate and overcome the challenges on your path to career advancement success. Let's consolidate your learnings with actionable steps, real-world success stories to inspire and guide you, and dive deeper into the Empowered Leadership Coaching Program to support your ongoing growth. There is so much more included in the program; this book just contains a few of the heavy hitters to help you get started.

Recap of the Three-Month Plan

Month 1: Laying the Foundation

- **Calendar Management:** Prioritize, delegate, consolidate, and eliminate tasks to create space for leadership activities.
- **Identify Your Value:** Complete the "50 Things I'm Most Proud Of" exercise and the Value Discovery Worksheet.
- **Craft Your Elevator Pitch:** Participate in the "10-Day Elevator Pitch Challenge" to refine your pitch.

Month 2: Building Momentum

- **Document Your Achievements:** Regularly update your achievements with metrics and specific examples.
- **Visibility Quest:** Start increasing your visibility through networking events, public speaking, and conducting informational interviews.
- **Seek Feedback:** Schedule one-on-one meetings with mentors and sponsors to discuss your progress and gather feedback.

Month 3: Solidifying Your Readiness

- **Update Your Resume and LinkedIn Profile:** Ensure your resume reflects your leadership experience and achievements. Update your LinkedIn profile to attract opportunities.

- **Practice Interview Skills:** Use the STAR format to prepare for common interview questions. Conduct mock interviews with a trusted colleague or coach.
- **Secure at Least 2 Mentors, Sponsors, or Coaches:** Start building your dream team of advisors who can help you move forward.

Summary of Key Actions

- **Calendar Management:** Ensure you allocate time for leadership activities, reflection, and preparation.
- **Visibility:** Increase your presence within your organization and industry by attending events, speaking, and networking.
- **Articulate Your Value:** Develop and practice your elevator pitch, update your resume, and prepare for interviews.
- **Seek Support:** Build a strong network of mentors, sponsors, and a coach to guide and support your journey.

Remember, asking for help is a power move and it will help you move forward faster. Why waste time trying to figure it out on your own?

Why Women Won't Ask for Help and How It Hurts Their Career Advancement

Many women struggle with asking for help, feeling that they must prove themselves by handling everything on their own. This mindset can be exhausting and detrimental to career advancement. Here's why:

- **Fear of Appearing Incompetent:** Women often fear that asking for help will be seen as a sign of weakness or incompetence. However, this reluctance can lead to burnout and missed opportunities for collaboration and growth.
- **Cultural Conditioning:** Societal expectations and gender norms can pressure women to be self-reliant and not show vulnerability. This conditioning can make it difficult to reach out for support.
- **Impact on Career:** Trying to do it all alone can hinder professional growth. Seeking help can lead to better performance, stronger relationships, and more visible leadership.
- **Exhaustion and Burnout:** Doing everything yourself is not sustainable. It leads to physical and mental exhaustion, which can impact productivity and overall career satisfaction.

Embracing the willingness to ask for help and leverage the support of others is crucial for sustainable career advancement.

Real-World Success Stories

Susan's Story: Owning Her Power and Earning a Promotion

Susan, a regional manager at a telecom company, felt stuck in her role. Despite her hard work, she wasn't getting the recognition she deserved. Through coaching, Susan learned to elevate her leadership, articulate her value effectively, and stand out as a promotion-ready leader. Within three months of starting her program, she confidently declared, "I feel like I've outgrown my job!" Susan's transformation included setting clear goals, managing her calendar strategically, and elevating her brand through visibility quests. This led to her promotion to Division Senior Manager. She also shared with me that her annual review was the best she had ever received.

Carla's Story: From Confused to Confident

Carla, a Director at a nonprofit, struggled with confidence. Promoted during the pandemic, Carla felt she hadn't fully grasped her new role and struggled with self-doubt. We worked on identifying her obstacles and creating a plan forward, focusing on time, mindset, and clarity. Carla freed up time on her calendar, boosting her confidence and leading to significant recognition from her peers and leaders. She is now thriving as a leader, making a significant impact in her role.

Amanda's Story: Rebuilding Confidence After a Setback

Amanda, a leader in a large corporation, lost her confidence after a mistake the prior year. This mistake wasn't completely her fault, but there was an unspoken expectation that she should take responsibility for it. The situation caused a lot of frustration. We worked on her goals, value articulation, and visibility quest. The best part of her visibility quest was that she found a community of women who had experienced similar situations, and those conversations reinforced her coaching and helped her gain even more courage. When the time was right, she had a transformative conversation with a key leader at her company who had been involved in the mistake. She took ownership, which cleared the line of communication and immediately rebuilt trust, confidence, and her brand. Amanda recently interviewed for a new Director role and felt more confident than ever, receiving compliments on her interview performance.

Luz's Story: Overcoming Imposter Syndrome and Stepping into Leadership

Luz, a Manager at a major tech company, constantly felt like an imposter despite her significant contributions and accomplishments. She couldn't understand why she wasn't getting ahead. Through the Empowered Leadership Coaching Program, we shifted her focus to leadership-level activities, including delegating some of the detailed work she was comfortable with. This shift helped build her self-confidence. As she started recognizing her true value, she became more comfortable having courageous conversations with leaders at her company. As Luz began to own her achievements, her visibility within the company increased. She took on high-profile projects, volunteered to mentor others, and built a strong network of supporters. Her newfound confidence and leadership presence have positioned her well for a promotion to Director.

Empowered Leadership Coaching Program

Does this sound like you?

- Overlooked for promotions despite working harder than any other candidate.
- Completing countless courses and education units, yet still not getting promoted.
- Taking on more responsibility, hoping your boss will notice.
- Frustrated with vague feedback like "you need more education".
- Doing double the work after a reorg with no additional compensation.
- Afraid that a past mistake has ruined your reputation.
- Recently promoted to Manager or Director, but have no idea of what you should be doing differently.

If you can relate, you're not alone. Many women face these challenges.

Introducing the Empowered Leadership Coaching Program

Achieve your career goals faster with the Empowered Leadership Coaching™ Group Program, designed to remove guesswork and provide proven strategies. These strategies have been successfully implemented in my own career and those of hundreds of other women. With 18 focused coaching modules and 12 full months of access, plus budget-friendly installment plans, our program is tailored for your success.

Program Highlights:

- **Set SMART Career Goals:** Define clear, achievable goals and create a strategic plan to reach them.
- **Demonstrate New Skills Immediately:** Apply new skills and strategies right away to stand out.
- **Elevate Your Professional Presence:** Build a strong personal brand that sets you apart.
- **Create a High-Performing Team Culture:** Learn how to cultivate and nurture a team that excels.

- **Apply and Interview with Confidence:** Prepare thoroughly for your next promotion with confidence.
- **Stand Out as the Obvious Candidate:** Master the strategies that make you the top choice for your dream job.

Outcomes:

- Stand out as a promotion-ready leader with a clear and actionable career roadmap.
- Implement proven strategies to eliminate guesswork and frustration.
- Transform into a confident, capable, and recognized leader in your field.

How to Join

Visit Empowered Leadership Coaching to learn more and apply.

Contact Information

For more information or questions, reach out to tabatha@ empowered-leader.com

Next Steps

Take the first step towards continuous growth and leadership excellence by joining the program today.

Final Motivational Message

Your journey toward career advancement is a continuous process of growth, learning, and adaptation. By applying the strategies and tools discussed in this book, you are taking proactive steps to ensure your success. Remember, the key to career growth is not just working hard, but working smart. It's about positioning yourself as a leader, showcasing your value, and being ready to seize opportunities as they arise.

You have the power to transform your career and achieve your goals. Believe in yourself, stay committed to your plan, and continue to seek opportunities for growth.

Chapter 13 Reflection

- What are the most important takeaways from this book, and how will you apply them to your career?
- How can you maintain the momentum of your career advancement journey and continue to grow as a leader?
- Reflect on your career goals. How have they evolved throughout this book, and what steps will you take next to achieve them?
- Reflect on what your future could look like if you have the support of a Career Advancement & Leadership Coach who's ready to help show you the way.

CHAPTER 14

Utilize Essential Tools and Resources for Career Success

Embarking on the journey to become promotion-ready and advance your career requires the right tools and resources. This chapter is your treasure chest of essential tools to help you stay organized, focused, and on track. These resources are designed to support the strategies and actions outlined in this book, making your career advancement journey more structured and effective.

Goal Setting Resource

Setting clear, actionable goals is the cornerstone of career advancement. This resource will guide you through creating SMART goals—Specific, Measurable, Achievable, Relevant, and Time-bound—that align with your long-term career aspirations. With well-defined objectives and a detailed action plan, you'll be able to measure your progress and stay motivated.

50 Things I'm Most Proud Of Resource

Reflecting on your accomplishments can boost your confidence and provide a clear understanding of your strengths. This resource encourages you to list fifty achievements, no matter how small, that you are proud of. This exercise not only reinforces your self-worth but also helps you identify patterns and skills that you can leverage in your career advancement.

Skills Inventory Resource

Knowing your skills is essential for identifying areas for growth and potential career opportunities. This resource helps you catalog your current skills and assess their relevance to your desired career path. By regularly updating your skills inventory, you can ensure that you are continuously developing in alignment with industry demands and personal career goals.

Networking Resource

Building and maintaining a robust professional network is vital for career progression. This resource provides strategies for effective networking, including tips on how to connect with industry leaders, colleagues, and potential mentors. It also offers templates for crafting engaging introduction messages and follow-up emails, ensuring you leave a positive impression.

Informational Interview Questions Resource

Informational interviews are a powerful tool for gaining insights into your desired career path and expanding your professional network. This resource offers a comprehensive list of questions to ask during these interviews, helping you gather valuable information and establish meaningful connections. By preparing thoughtful questions, you'll demonstrate your interest and eagerness to learn, making a lasting impression on industry professionals.

Conclusion

This toolkit is designed to support your journey toward becoming promotion-ready and advancing your career. By utilizing these resources, you will stay organized, maintain focus, and continuously progress toward your goals. Remember, career advancement is a continuous process of learning, growing, and adapting. Stay committed, be proactive, and leverage these tools to unlock your full potential.

If you have questions or want to learn more about the Empowered Leadership Coaching Program and whether it would be a great fit for you, please reach out via email at Tabatha@Empowered-leader.com. Your journey to career success begins with the right tools and a strategic plan—let's make it happen!

GOAL SETTING

Setting clear, actionable goals is fundamental to career success. The SMART criteria—Specific, Measurable, Achievable, Relevant, and Time-bound—provides a reliable framework for defining your goals and tracking your progress.

Use a simple Google Doc or Excel spreadsheet to set and review your goals regularly, adjusting as needed to stay on track. The more specific you are, the easier it is to track your achievements.

Pro Tip: Use your calendar to tie smaller steps within your goals to a tighter timeline.

SMART Goal Setting:

- **Specific:** Clearly define what you want to achieve.
- **Measurable:** Determine how you will measure success.

- **Achievable:** Ensure your goal is realistic and attainable.
- **Relevant:** Align your goal with your broader career objectives.
- **Time-bound:** Set a deadline for achieving your goal.

Example:

- **Specific:** I will prepare for a promotion to the Director level by developing key leadership skills, expanding my professional network, and enhancing my visibility within the company.
- **Measurable:** I will track my progress by setting specific deliverables, such as updating my resume by the end of January, conducting at least two informational interviews per month, attending four networking events by June, and completing a leadership development course by August.
- **Achievable:** I will create space in my schedule by adjusting my calendar, delegating non-essential tasks, consolidating meetings, and eliminating low-priority commitments. This will allow me to focus on professional development and career advancement activities.
- **Relevant:** This goal aligns with my career aspirations and prepares me for the next promotion opportunity by ensuring that I have

the necessary skills, experience, and visibility within the company.

- **Time-bound:** I will complete all these activities and be fully prepared for a Director-level promotion by (specific date).

By following the SMART framework, you can set clear and actionable goals that will propel your career forward. Regularly review and adjust your goals to stay aligned with your career path and ensure continuous progress. Remember, goal setting is an ongoing process that requires dedication and proactive management.

SMART Goal Setting Template

Component	Description	Your Goal
Specific	Clearly define what you want to achieve.	
Measurable	Determine how you will measure success.	
Achievable	Ensure your goal is realistic and attainable.	
Relevant	Align your goal with your broader career objectives.	
Time-bound	Set a deadline for achieving your goal.	
Additional Notes	Any additional notes or steps.	

50 Things I'm Most Proud Of

This exercise is designed to boost your confidence and help you recognize and track your unique value and achievements. By regularly documenting your successes, you'll have a ready list of accomplishments to refer to during performance reviews, job interviews, and promotion discussions. It's also a great reminder of how amazing you are and can be used as a reference any time you need a quick pick-me-up.

Start by creating a Google Doc or Excel spreadsheet with 50 lines and capture anything that's important to you. For career-related successes, make sure you capture metrics whenever possible. Regularly update this list with new accomplishments and review it often to remind yourself of your value and capabilities.

Tips for Success:

- **Be Specific:** The more detailed you are, the more impactful your list will be.
- **Include Metrics:** Quantify your achievements where possible to highlight your impact.
- **Reflect Regularly:** Make it a habit to update your list and reflect on your accomplishments.

Here are a few things that are on my list to inspire you:

- I rescued my last two dogs and gave them amazing lives.
- I've helped 100's of clients and connections build confidence in themselves.
- I've changed the lives of people who were struggling in their careers.
- I've raised an amazing son with an entrepreneurial mind.
- I helped my husband launch a very successful remodeling business in 2005.

- I became 100% debt-free at the age of 48.
- I completed the largest billing system migration in the history of my company as a project manager.
- I consistently achieved high scores on employee survey results, exceeding the company average by 1.7%.
- I led a team of 400 people across 40+ states through a massive reorganization effort with zero job losses.
- I'm a great friend, always willing to listen to others with empathy.
- I'm an outstanding coach; most of my clients have become friends.
- 100% of my direct reports were promoted during the last reorganization.
- I'm friends with all of my former direct reports.
- One of my clients, Janus, told me "You were sent from God to LinkedIn on the exact day I needed you most."
- I volunteer, delivering food to people in need in my neighborhood, having a positive impact on their lives (and mine)

When you get stuck, ask close family, friends, and colleagues for help. We both know you've done some amazing things. Don't overthink it—just start writing!

Please complete a list of 50 things you are most proud of. Think about career accomplishments, life accomplishments, lives you've impacted, etc. There are no wrong answers. *For Career Accomplishments please include Stats/Metrics where possible.

1
2
3
4
5
6
7
8
9
10
11
12
13
14
15
16
17
18
19
20
21
22
23
24
25
26
27
28
29
30
31
32
33
34
35
36
37
38
39
40
41
42
43
44
45
46
47
48
49
50

Skills Inventory - Value Discovery Worksheet

Understanding your skills and unique value proposition is essential for articulating your strengths and identifying areas for growth. This simple exercise will help you document your skills, experiences, and the value you bring to your organization.

Grab a Google Doc or Excel Spreadsheet and get to work. Use separate columns for each category.

Skills Inventory - Value Discovery Worksheet:

- **Core Skills:**
  List your key skills here. Be specific and consider both hard and soft skills.
- **Experience:**
  Detail your relevant experience. Include job titles, responsibilities, and the duration of each role.
- **Achievements:**
  Highlight significant achievements. Mention awards, recognitions, or projects you successfully completed.
- **Unique Selling Points:**
  Identify what sets you apart from others. Focus on your unique strengths and qualities.
- **Impact Metrics:**
  Include quantifiable results, such as time

saved, revenue generated, percentage improvements, etc. These metrics showcase your contributions and impact.

Use this worksheet to prepare for performance reviews, job interviews, networking, elevator pitch creation, and career planning sessions. Regularly update it to reflect your growth and new accomplishments.

By thoroughly documenting your skills and experiences, you'll have a comprehensive overview of your professional value. This not only boosts your confidence but also equips you with the information needed to communicate your unique value effectively in any career-related situation.

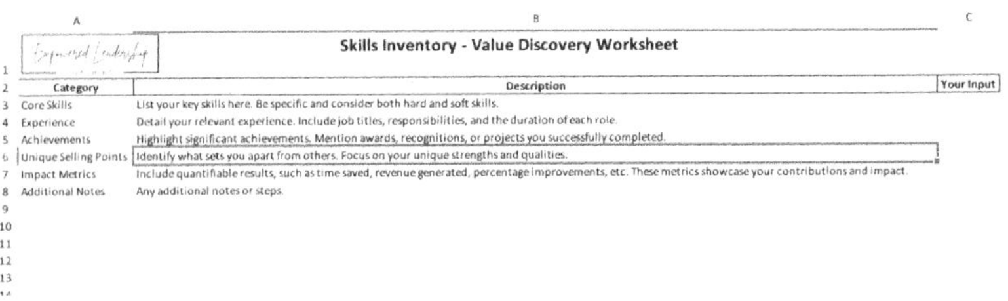

Skills Inventory - Value Discovery Worksheet

Category	Description	Your Input
Core Skills	List your key skills here. Be specific and consider both hard and soft skills.	
Experience	Detail your relevant experience. Include job titles, responsibilities, and the duration of each role.	
Achievements	Highlight significant achievements. Mention awards, recognitions, or projects you successfully completed.	
Unique Selling Points	Identify what sets you apart from others. Focus on your unique strengths and qualities.	
Impact Metrics	Include quantifiable results, such as time saved, revenue generated, percentage improvements, etc. These metrics showcase your contributions and impact.	
Additional Notes	Any additional notes or steps.	

Do not forget your leadership skills:

Experience Inventory

General Core Competencies/Skills.

- Customer Experience
- Communication
- Teamwork
- Employee Experience
- Diversity & Inclusion
- Problem-solving
- Adaptability
- Time management
- Attention to detail
- Customer service
- Interpersonal skills
- Technical proficiency
- Organizational skills
- Critical thinking
- Conflict resolution
- Creativity and innovation
- Team Leadership
- Decision-making
- Empathy
- Professionalism
- Analytical skills
- Project management
- Negotiation
- Financial acumen
- Presentation skills
- Technical (Insert specific)
- Change management
- Strategic thinking
- Budget Management
- Research skills
- Collaboration
- Crisis Management
- Data analysis
- Multi-Lingual (languages)
- Meeting facilitation
- Mentoring
- Report writing
- Public speaking
- Risk management
- Safety Compliance
- Cross-functional leadership
- Vendor Relations
- Sales
- Process improvement
- Compliance
- Continuous Improvement
- Strategic Planning
- Resource Management

Networking Tracker - My Fan Club

Building and maintaining a strong professional network is vital for career advancement. This tracker helps you keep tabs on your connections, including mentors, sponsors, colleagues, and new contacts made through networking events. By organizing your contacts and tracking interactions, you can ensure you maintain and nurture these valuable relationships.

Start a new Google Doc or Excel Spreadsheet and create the following columns to begin:

Networking Tracker - My Fan Club:Example:

Name	Jane Doe
Position	Senior Marketing Manager
Organization	XYZ Corp
Connection Date	March 15, 2024
Follow-up Date	April 15, 2024
Notes	Met at ABC Conference, discussed digital marketing trends and potential collaborations.

Tips for Using Your Networking Tracker:

- **Be Detailed:** The more information you record about each interaction, the easier it will be to pick up the conversation later.
- **Set Reminders:** Use calendar alerts to remind you of follow-up dates.
- **Stay Consistent:** Regularly update your tracker to reflect new connections and interactions.
- **Personalize Follow-ups:** Mention previous conversations or shared interests to strengthen the relationship.

By maintaining an organized and up-to-date networking tracker, you can effectively manage your professional relationships, ensuring you stay connected and engaged with your network.

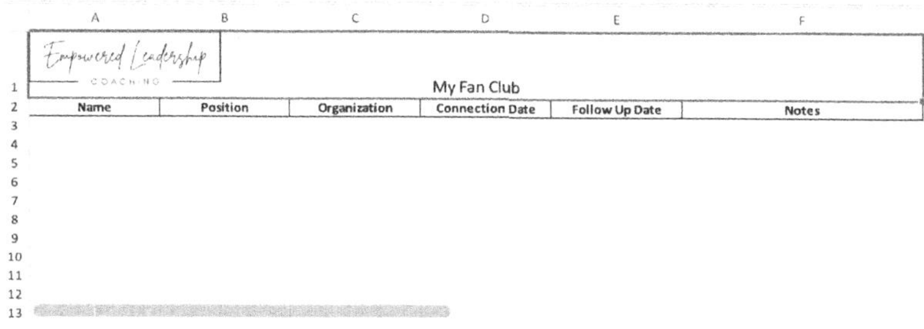

My Fan Club

Name	Position	Organization	Connection Date	Follow Up Date	Notes

Informational Interview Questions

Conducting informational interviews is a powerful strategy to gain insights into your desired role and industry. Prepare thoughtful questions to make the most of these opportunities, and take notes so you can personalize your follow-up messages and conversations.

General Questions

- Can you tell me about your current role and responsibilities?
- How did you get started in your career, and what led you to this position?
- What does a typical day look like for you?
- What are the biggest challenges you face in your role?
- What do you enjoy most about your job?

Career Path and Development

- What career path did you take to get to your current position?
- What skills and experiences have been most important in your career progression?
- How do you see your career evolving in the next 5-10 years?
- What advice would you give someone looking to advance their career in this field?
- Can you recommend any resources (books, courses, certifications) that have been particularly helpful to you?

Company Culture and Values

- How would you describe the company culture here?
- What do you think are the core values of our organization?
- How does the company support professional development and growth?
- Can you share an example of a project or initiative that embodies the company's values?
- What is the best way to get involved in company culture and activities?

Department and Team Insights

- Can you tell me more about your department's goals and objectives?

- How does your team collaborate and communicate effectively?
- What are the key performance indicators (KPIs) for your department?
- What recent projects or initiatives has your team worked on?
- How does your department contribute to the overall success of the company?

Leadership and Management

- How would you describe your leadership style?
- What qualities do you believe make an effective leader?
- Can you share a time when you had to overcome a significant leadership challenge?
- How do you motivate and inspire your team?
- What is your approach to managing conflict within the team?

Skills and Competencies

- What technical skills are most important for success in your role?
- How do you stay updated with the latest industry trends and developments?
- What soft skills do you believe are crucial for career advancement?
- How do you approach problem-solving and decision-making in your role?

- What tools or technologies do you use most frequently in your work?

Personal Growth and Balance

- How do you balance work and personal life?
- What strategies do you use to manage stress and maintain productivity?
- Can you share a personal achievement that you're particularly proud of?
- How do you set and achieve your personal development goals?
- What hobbies or activities do you enjoy outside of work?

Networking and Visibility

- How do you build and maintain professional relationships within the company?
- What advice do you have for someone looking to increase their visibility in the organization?
- Can you recommend any internal groups or networks that are beneficial to join?
- How do you approach networking at company events and meetings?
- Who are some key people you think I should connect with in the company?

Future Opportunities and Advice

- What upcoming projects or initiatives are you most excited about?
- What do you see as the biggest opportunities for growth in our industry?
- How do you foresee the company evolving in the next few years?
- What trends do you think will impact our industry the most in the near future?
- What do you wish you had known when you were starting out in your career?

Mentorship and Sponsorship

- Who have been your most influential mentors and why?
- What qualities do you look for in a mentor?
- How do you find and cultivate mentorship relationships?
- What role has mentorship played in your career development?
- Can you provide advice on how to seek out sponsorship within the organization?

Career Advancement Questions

- What strengths do you look for when hiring a leader on your team?

- Can you describe a recent successful leadership promotion within the company and what made that individual stand out?
- What are the most important experiences or projects that you believe contribute to a successful career progression here?
- How does the company identify and develop high-potential employees for leadership roles?
- What advice would you give to someone looking to advance to a leadership position within the next few years?

Use these questions as a starting point and tailor them to fit the specific context of each interview. Taking detailed notes during your informational interviews will allow you to personalize your follow-ups and maintain meaningful connections.

An Invitation to Continue Your Journey with Promotion Ready in 3 Months Bootcamp

Unlock Your Leadership Potential with Our Intensive Group Coaching Program

Congratulations on taking the first step toward advancing your career with "Promotion Ready in 3 Months: The Women's Career Advancement Guide." But don't stop here—take your journey to the next level with our exclusive **Promotion Ready in 3 Months Bootcamp**.

Why Join Our Bootcamp?

1. Strategic Career Guidance

Receive expert advice from Tabatha Jones, a seasoned career coach who understands the unique challenges women face in the workplace.

2. Empowering Community

Connect with a powerful network of like-minded women who are equally committed to advancing their careers. Share experiences, gain insights, and find encouragement within a supportive community.

3. Proven, Practical Strategies

Access the practical tools and techniques featured in "Promotion Ready in 3 Months." These strategies have helped countless women unlock their leadership potential and land their dream jobs

4. Accountability and Motivation

Stay on track with regular check-ins and progress updates. The group setting fosters a sense of accountability and keeps you motivated to achieve your goals.

5. Flexible and Accessible

This bootcamp is designed for ambitious women ready to take immediate action. Participate in live sessions focused on practical exercises that deliver real, lasting results.

What You'll Gain:

- **Confidence:** Build genuine confidence that comes from knowing your worth and capabilities.
- **Visibility:** Learn how to elevate your professional presence and stand out in your field.
- **Leadership Skills:** Develop the essential skills needed to lead effectively and authentically.
- **Career Advancement:** Create a clear, actionable plan for achieving your next promotion.

Ready to Take the Next Step?

Don't let your journey end here. Join our **Promotion Ready in 3 Months Bootcamp** and unlock your full potential as a confident, capable, and recognized leader. Scan the QR code to register today!!

Contact Us

If you have any questions or need more information, feel free to visit my website at www.empowered-leader.com or reach out to me directly at tabatha@empowered-leader.com. I'm here to support you and cheer you on every step of the way.

BTW-If you love podcasts, be sure to like and follow "Empowered Leadership Coaching with Tabatha" on Apple and/or Spotify.

Empowered Leadership Coaching™ – Empowering Women, Transforming Careers.

ABOUT THE AUTHOR

Tabatha Jones is a dynamic Career Advancement and Leadership Coach, keynote speaker, podcaster, and author with over 20 years of leadership experience in corporate America. Having successfully navigated the corporate ladder and transitioned to entrepreneurship at 50, she now dedicates her expertise to empowering women to achieve their career goals.

Tabatha's journey is marked by her passion for helping women overcome the challenges she once faced—self-doubt, missed opportunities, and the frustration of being overlooked for promotions. Her experiences ignited her commitment to guide women in navigating their careers more strategically and effectively.

Through her exclusive Empowered Leadership Coaching Program, Tabatha has guided countless women to unlock their leadership potential, secure promotions and land new jobs. Her program is designed to help women become more powerfully positioned as promotion-ready leaders, with practical strategies and a focus on continuous growth.

Tabatha's dedication extends beyond individual coaching. She creates a supportive community where women can share their journeys, learn from each other, and celebrate their successes. Her approach is rooted in the belief that small, consistent actions lead to significant career advancements.

By following the strategies and insights in this book, you are taking the first step towards transforming your career. Let Tabatha's guidance help you navigate the path to becoming a confident, capable, and recognized leader in your field.